MW01621127

TOMOKAZU MATSUYAMA

TOMOKAZU MATSUYAMA

Found Modern Library

FIFTY24SF

INTRODUCTION BY ALEXANDRA CHANG

PHOTOGRAPHY BY GION
NAOBUMI CHIBA
YUSUKE WAKABAYASHI

TOMOKAZU MATSUYAMA:
AN ORGANIC COSMOPOLITANISM

BY ALEXANDRA CHANG

> At the center of Tomokazu Matsuyama's art wrestles the notion of an überculture—one splashed in Technicolor, struggling with the apparent chaos of a progressively ever more cosmopolitan urban life. As in urban metropolitan settings, in the worlds of Matsuyama's paintings various icons of cultural meaning touch as non-sensically yet remain as commonplace as a Coca-Cola bottle set on a table in a sushi restaurant in Williamsburg, NY. Or in the case of Matsuyama's installation ***Leonora Music Vox*** (2006): an installation of a large, yet toy-like wind-up house set amid a Tokyo gallery with a video of his elderly neighbor and quintessential Brooklynite, Leonora, peering out a side window. Through these apparently randomized points of contact between wandering cultural signifiers, the artist investigates the nebulous overlapping space of seemingly common bipolar dichotomies including design and art, East and West, contemporary and traditional, and order and chaos. And instead of individual elements of form and content, he finds within their muddied borders and connections, an organic chaos.

In Matsuyama's work ***Kirin*** (2006), the artist uproots the traditionally revered symbolic image of the well-known mythological creature symbolizing "prosperity" and instead figures it amid an abstract white space, dripping in a bright contemporary acrylic color palette, with a fumbling character in Western garb trying to climb up on its back. The artist is well aware that the artwork is being viewed within a U.S. art market in which the original iconic cultural meaning of the kirin will be lost. Instead with the icon of the kirin, the artist questions this shift of meaning he has reappropriated with the image now rearing its mythic head in a randomized and patchwork international setting outside of its original culture. For Matsuyama, the artwork, while appearing to be enmeshed in a chaos of internationalism is in fact natural and at aesthetic ease in its cosmopolitanism.

In his work ***Unit*** (2006) and ***Shunger*** (2006), the artist appropriates images that originate in Japan's Edo period ***ukiyo-e*** woodblock prints of beautiful women, ***Bijin-Ga***, as well as of the exquisite artistry of the spring pictures, ***Shun-Ga***. The ***Shun-Ga*** prints feature sexual encounters using a complex 10-block multicolor technique. These two pieces demonstrate Matsuyama's research in traditional woodblock prints and textiles that stem from a childhood spent in the traditional city of Takayama, Japan, where these age-old industries still exist, and his past as a graphic designer with an interest in contemporary patterns and colors. In ***Shunger*** the artist plays with modern polka dots and striped patterns paired with heaps of overflowing fabric, arms and legs, taken directly out of a combination of Toyokuni's works portraying highly emotive characters caught amid their sexual exploits. Matsuyama is able to re-situate the characters of an intimately tangled couple and man bending backwards and remix them into a contemporary international mélange of icons and patterns, thereby losing the original sense of the piece and its cultural belonging as a traditional Japanese erotic print and instead consciously placing them into the inter-textual world of contemporary conceptual art.

The artist's heightened awareness of randomized international overlaps and fluidity as well as highly acute consciousness of his own contemporary art aesthetic stem from Matsuyama's background as a graphic designer and earlier works based in the urban subculture of street-influenced artwork. In January 2002, Matsuyama came to New York City after spending his childhood weaving back and forth from the mountains of Takayama and Orange County, L.A. He also left behind a professional career in snowboarding in Japan. Breaking both his ankles in a bad fall that left him in the hospital for a month and unable to walk for 10 months, he found another creative outlet through art during his recovery. His designs would soon find their way to snowboard lines and clothing and his artwork would be featured in ***Dazed and Confused***, Japan, among other street art culture magazines, as street-influenced artwork and design began to swell into mainstream popularity.

Returning to the U.S., Matsuyama landed in New York City directly after 9/11, where cultural awareness in a cosmopolitan urban setting became underlined due to the U.S. led war on terror. Matsuyama decided to dub himself Matzu-MTP, hoping to erase his identity as a Japanese artist and instead produce questioning around his "aka" identity. As a child and teenager growing up on both sides of the Pacific, Matsuyama had often described the everyday discrimination he felt in being both too Americanized and too Japanese. In the art market, his works were scrutinized and labeled as street-influenced or design. In his work ***Minority*** (2004), Matsuyama painted his alter ego as the Japanese icon of the goose, an animal that is used as a side character, but never the main subject of an artwork. His works would increasingly strive to meld his Japanese influences with his American influences of contemporary modern art, street, and design work.

As quickly as Matsuyama acquired the pseudonym Matzu-MTP, it seemed to take hold in the street-influenced art world through his telltale iconographies composed of what he termed the "reluctant worrier." The "worrier" character developed from Matsuyama's youthful reflections as a rebellious yet sympathetic commentary on male conformity and strain of responsibility in Japanese everyday life.

From early 2000 through 2004, the character of the "reluctant worrier" would appear in the artist's works, whether as a main subject of his pieces or as a side character. The character is a caricature of crossing lines that create a wrinkled face. During this time, Matsuyama's works varied from large-scaled multi-canvas font-based works such as ***Reluctant*** (2003) to ***It Ain't Easy to Love Your Foe*** (2003). The latter piece is made of six canvases, which combine Matsuyama's earlier use of letter forms and elements of design along with an exaggerated play with negative space, painted drips with edges that border on near-stencil perfection and the presence of his "reluctant worrier" faces masked into the lettering "F-O-E", each on a separate canvas. The piece resonates from the time, emerging from his street-graffiti influence, through his personal history of growing up under the advice of his father, a Protestant pastor. Also melding feelings of juvenile injustice and cultural difference experienced in the schoolyard to the atmosphere of war overcast in post 9/11 New York City, the piece was a patchwork quilt of sorts, pieced together with the intermingling yet disparate variations playing out their individual themes within a single artwork.

It was not long before Matsuyama soon found it difficult to concentrate solely on the "reluctant worrier" iconography that had become so familiar, he would often refer to the renderings as his "uncles." The icons in his work, including the worrier, his controlled drips, his stylized color palette of muted natural tones and bright yellow, his letter forms and numbers soon became his trademarks. However, because of these recurring elements in his work, Matsuyama found them too predictable, limiting his capacity to move outside of their scope. Style and creativity buckled into a conflict between remaining true to craft and loyalty to an established art audience.

During these years from 2000-2005, street-influenced artwork permeated mainstream galleries and museums, and street-influenced design became commonplace in museum shops. Design and art's overlap was being embraced by the fine art world. In December 2004, Matsuyama, still dubbed Matzu-MTP would co-curate an exhibit: "The Shift Exhibition," in which design and art were indistinguishably intertwined. The exhibition consisted of eight conceptual artworks created by eight artists with street-influenced backgrounds. Each of the artworks was created in the medium of a bike. Instead of reconstructing the bikes, the bike itself, in its form and functionality of a working bike design, was reconstituted into artwork medium and moving canvas.

At this juncture, two parallel conflicts arose for the artist concerning the very core of his being due to what the artist self-described as an identity crisis. The first grew from his concern that his work be seen not as a work by a Japanese artist or an Asian artist living in the U.S., but as an artist. The other concerned his place as an artist who straddled the line of fine art and what was seen as low art, or street-influenced art and design.

Defining his artist name as Matzu-MTP, as an icon or logo to brand himself became a heavy question for Matsuyama, for whom name and label proved categorizing entrapments from which he hoped to free himself and his artwork. Matsuyama found influences in Andy Warhol, who both changed his last name and also came from a commercial art background. He also became unable to paint at this time and instead brooded for months over medium, concept, and style. He increasingly looked to modern and contemporary artists such as Jeff Koons and Takashi Murakami for their ability to use pop cultural items as conceptual art. He also turned to researching and adopting key figures in modern art such as Claude Monet, Pablo Picasso and Jackson Pollock as those who broke the mold to shape influences in both his work and thought processes about his work.

In the summer of 2005, Matsuyama freed himself from a half a year of creative paralysis and struggle with style, medium and content with the show "In Situ Matzu-MTP: Exterior/Interior exhibition" (2005). In the exhibition, his work combining what he termed "a new visual language" or fusion of Eastern and Western influences, Matsuyama crossed fine art and design elements and contemporary and traditional themes. The exhibition itself was a comment on the circulation of the many elements of the highly mixed and growing artistic community in Williamsburg, Brooklyn. He created the interior wallpaper, wall installation, lightboxes, and acrylic on paper painting for the inside of the Brooklyn lounge Triple Crown. Outside on the street, he created murals including a 30-foot long piece showcasing the icons of the swan and monkey. On the metro stop to the lounge, he also designed a billboard showcasing an acrylic and paper piece that also featured the swan icon. For the artist, the intermingling of his artwork, the music of the lounge, and the people inside and outside in the community produced the natural order of the circulation of these multiple urban elements.

During this time, the figures of the swan, turtle, monkey and hunter appeared in his work. "Asian culture is being so hunted," explained Matsuyama of the interest that mainstream culture seemed to have on fusion and a renewed Orientalism towards film, food, and fashion among other popular elements of everyday life. He also continued with his use of numbers 0, 1, 2, 3, and 4, which had remained from his interest in typography. The numbers represent the idea of reincarnation for the artist, with "4" symbolic of death in Japan, and "0" and "1" meaning birth and reincarnation in the Japanese Buddhist tradition. By combining these ideas, the artist arranged several groupings of these numbers in his works, seemingly haphazardly and connected by lines, representing the order and chaos of life and reincarnation.

During the half-year of brooding over his work, Matsuyama began to utilize an acrylic on heavy watercolor paper technique that combined controlled paint splatters and heavy solid painted areas, which show the artist's mastery of his medium. The splashes of colors can be mistaken for watercolors, while other strokes can seem as solid as gold leaf. Continuing with this newfound medium, the artist began intense research into Modern art history as well as Japanese *ukiyo-e* prints. The result is his latest works created in 2006 that reappropriate characters from these traditional prints such as *Shunger*, *Kirin*, and *Unit*.

In these works, as well as *She-She*, *3rip-hors*, *Running* and *Summer-Talk*, the palette Matsuyama utilizes is brilliant with reds, blues, greens, oranges, and the composition of the frame is positioned off to the side, allowing for the focus of the artwork to be shifted to the side, a common practice in traditional Japanese prints. In *Summer-Talk* and *3rip-hors* this is taken to the extreme, where in the former, two characters are practically falling off the page and in the latter, the artist has decided to only take three side characters from a large-format print of a whole town's activities. Yet, again he has taken the characters of the traditional prints away from their original ether and placed them in the middle of fields of white or non-descript patterns. There is a story that they tell, but they are ambiguous, focused on what is outside the main point of view and lost from their original intended myths and cultural belonging.

In a similar vein, like his paintings the artist sits at the side amid an equally non-descript international überculture in which he is able to consciously state: *"I am not a Japanese artist, I am a modern artist that is Japanese."*

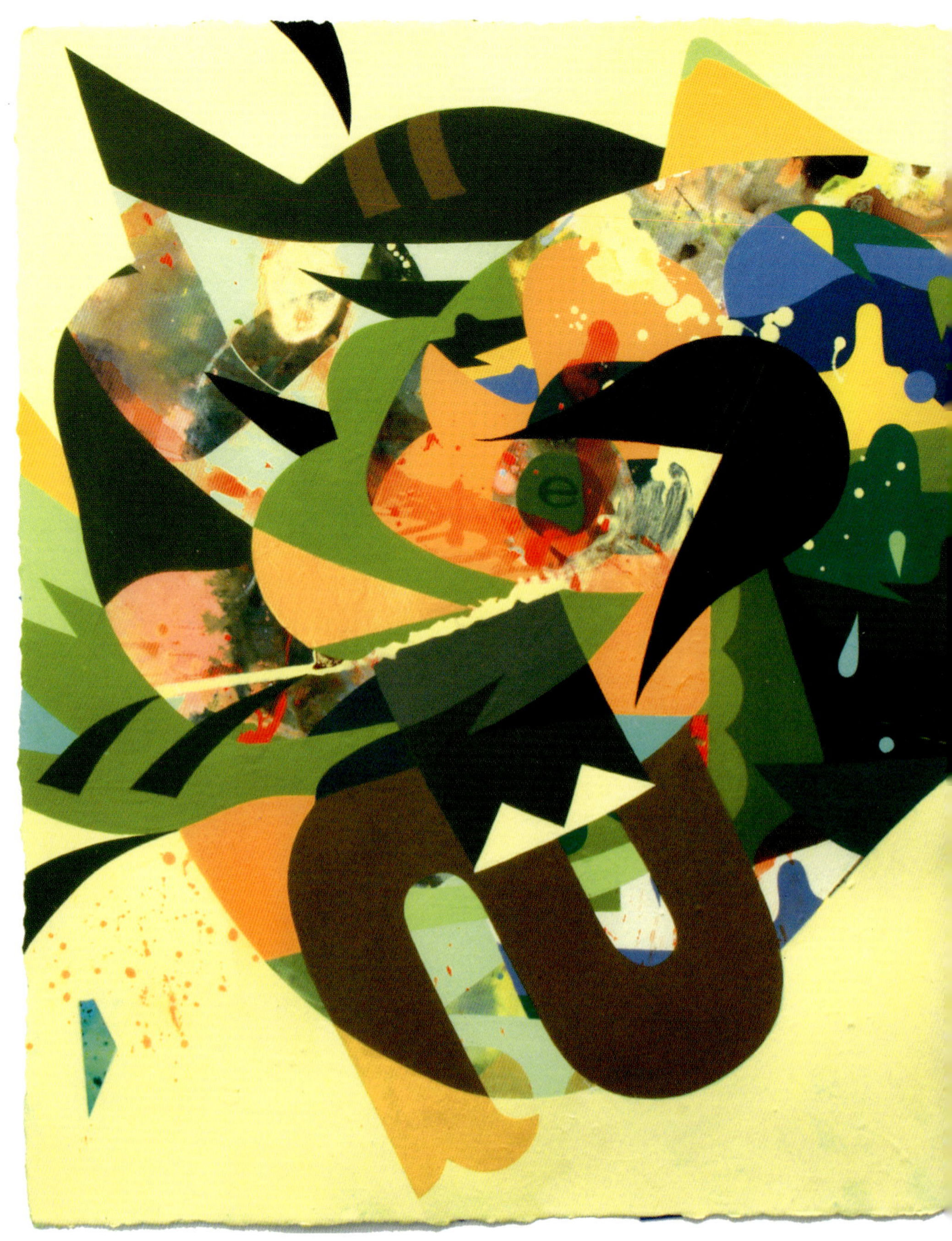

Exploray, 2005
Acrylic on paper
28 x 43"

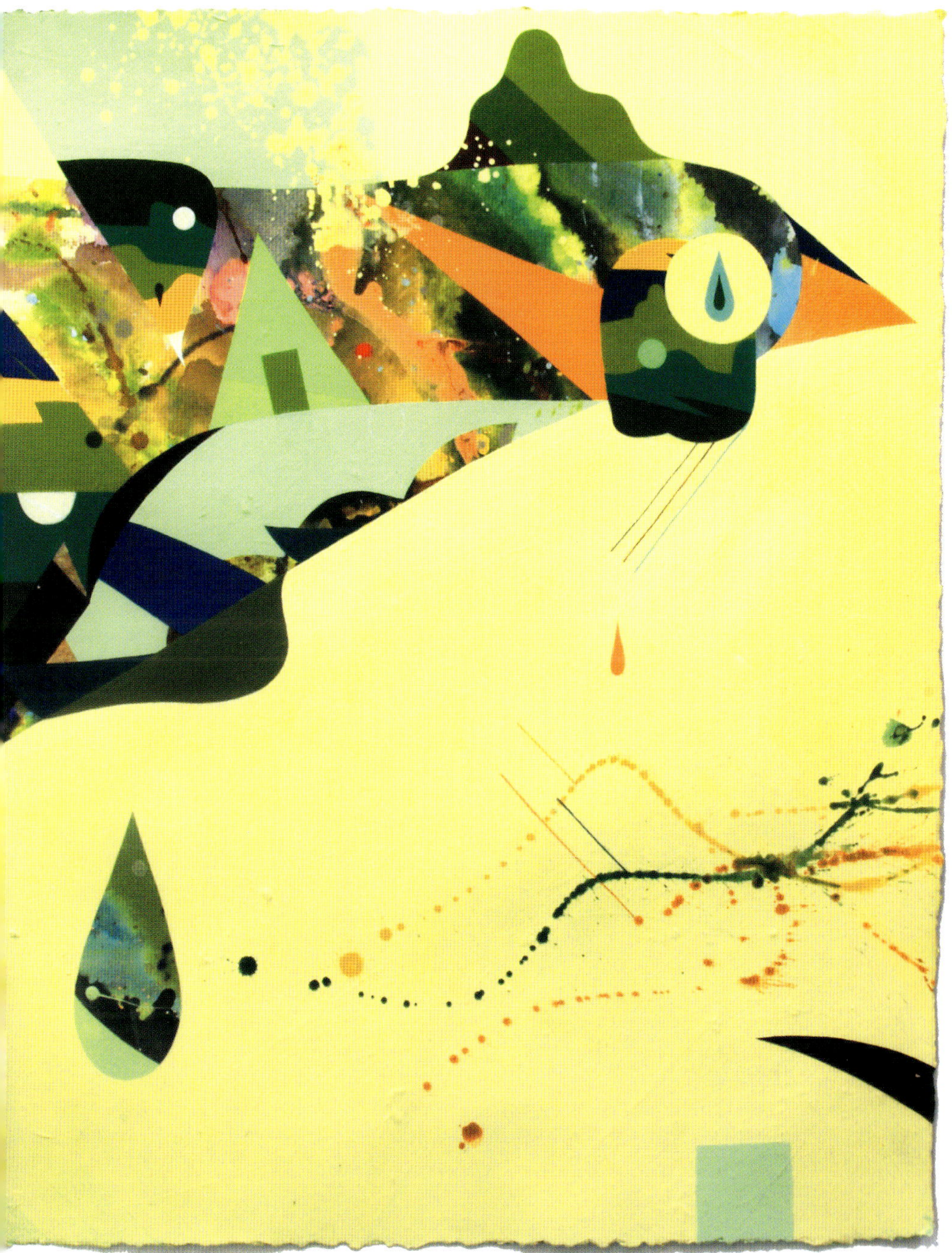

She-She, 2006
Acrylic on paper
20 x 15"

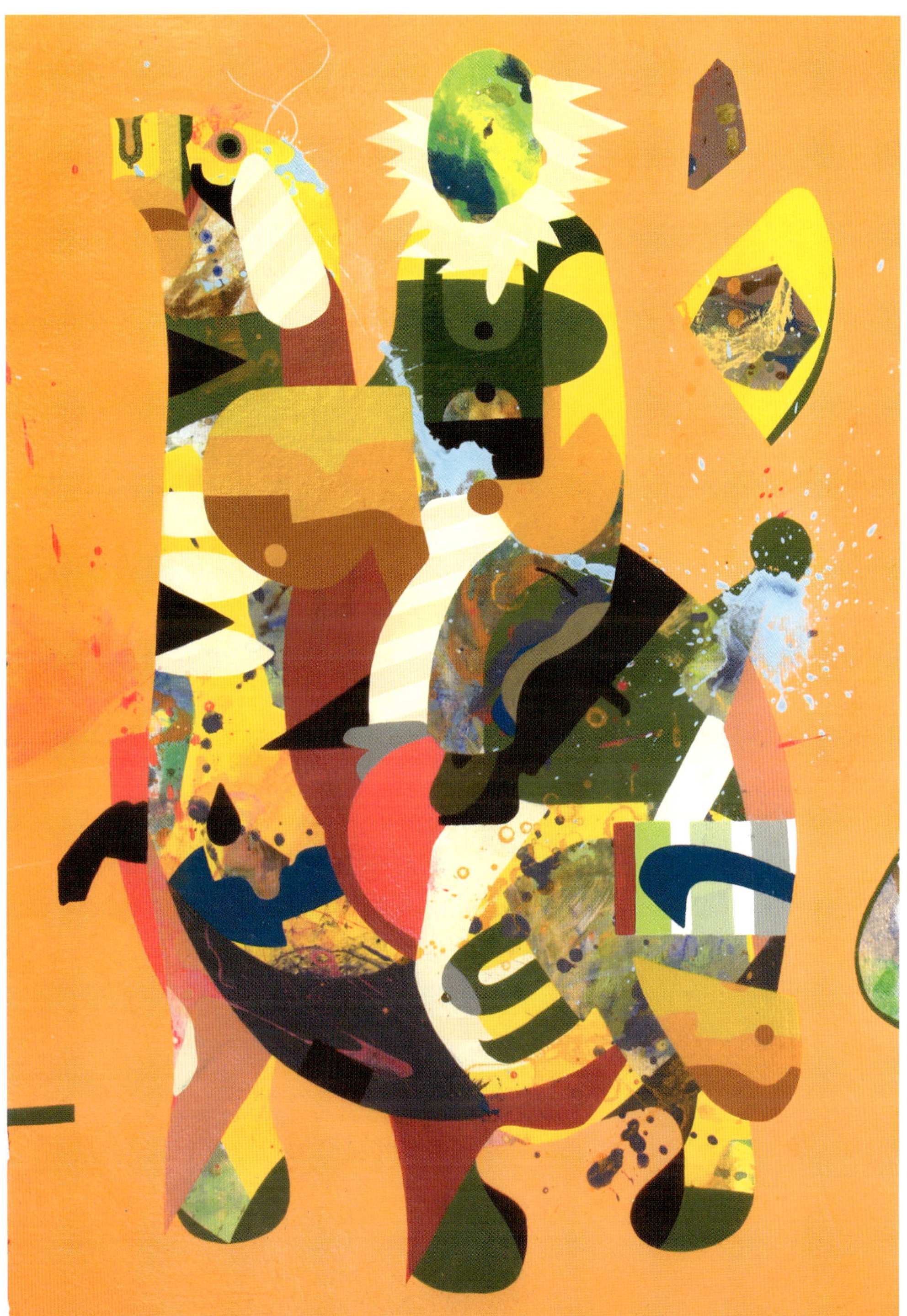

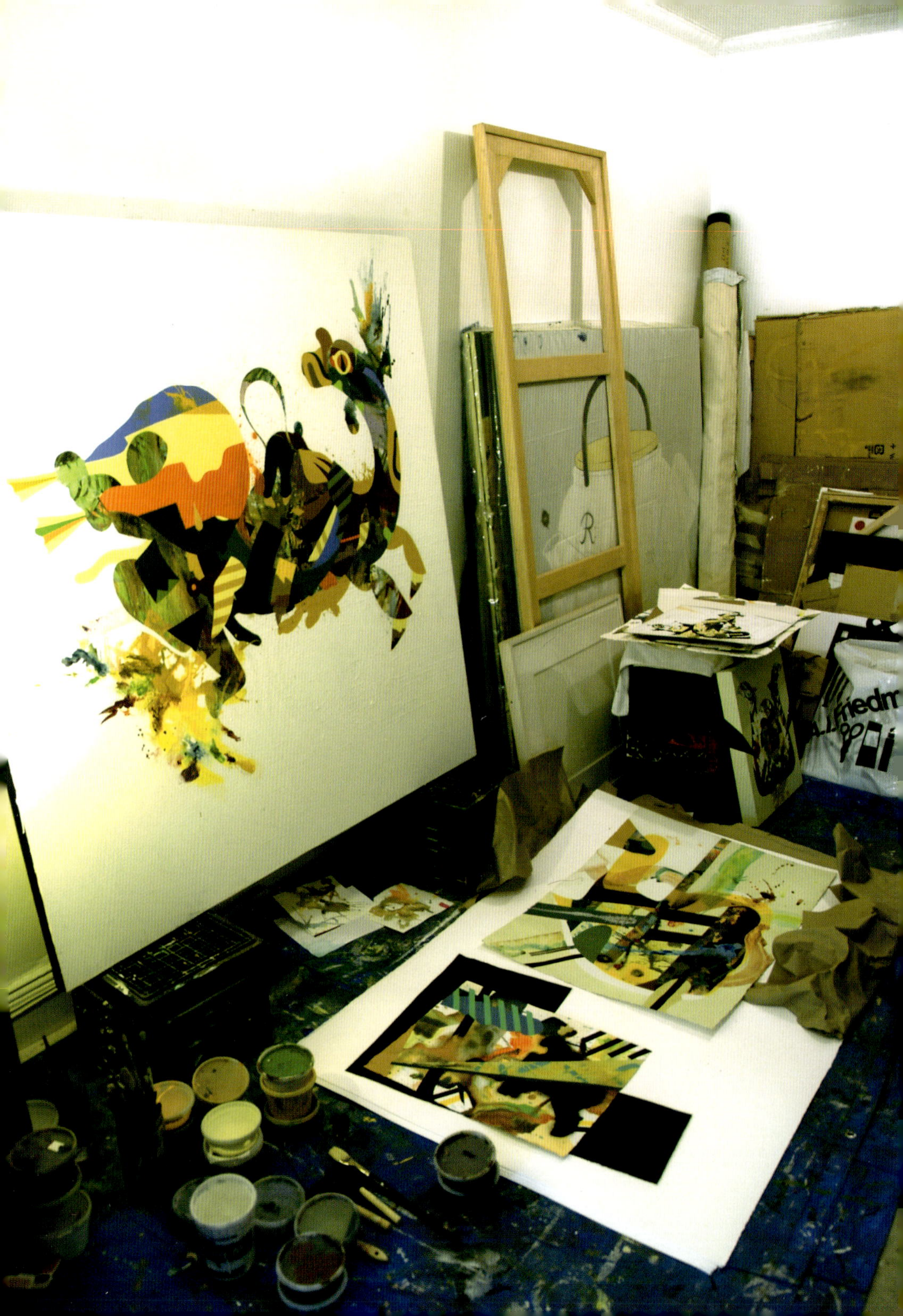

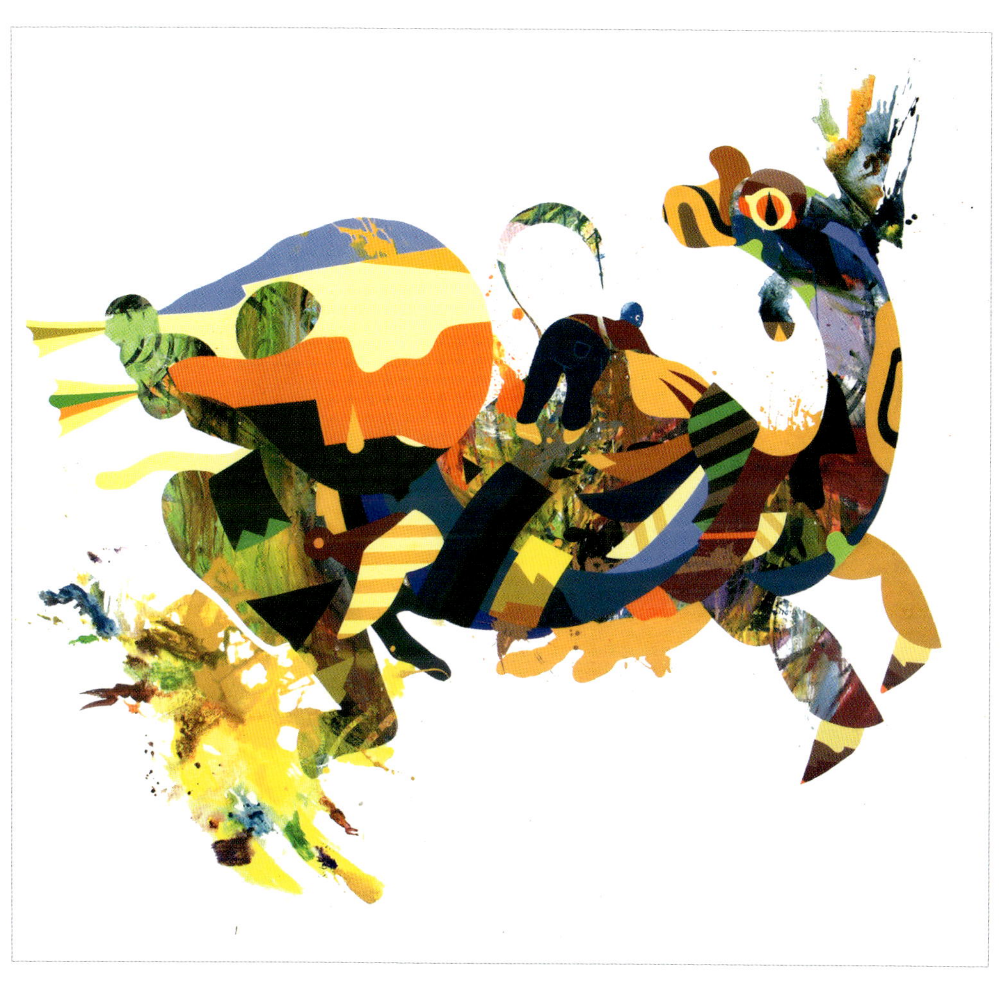

Kirin, 2006
Acrylic on canvas
60 x 60"

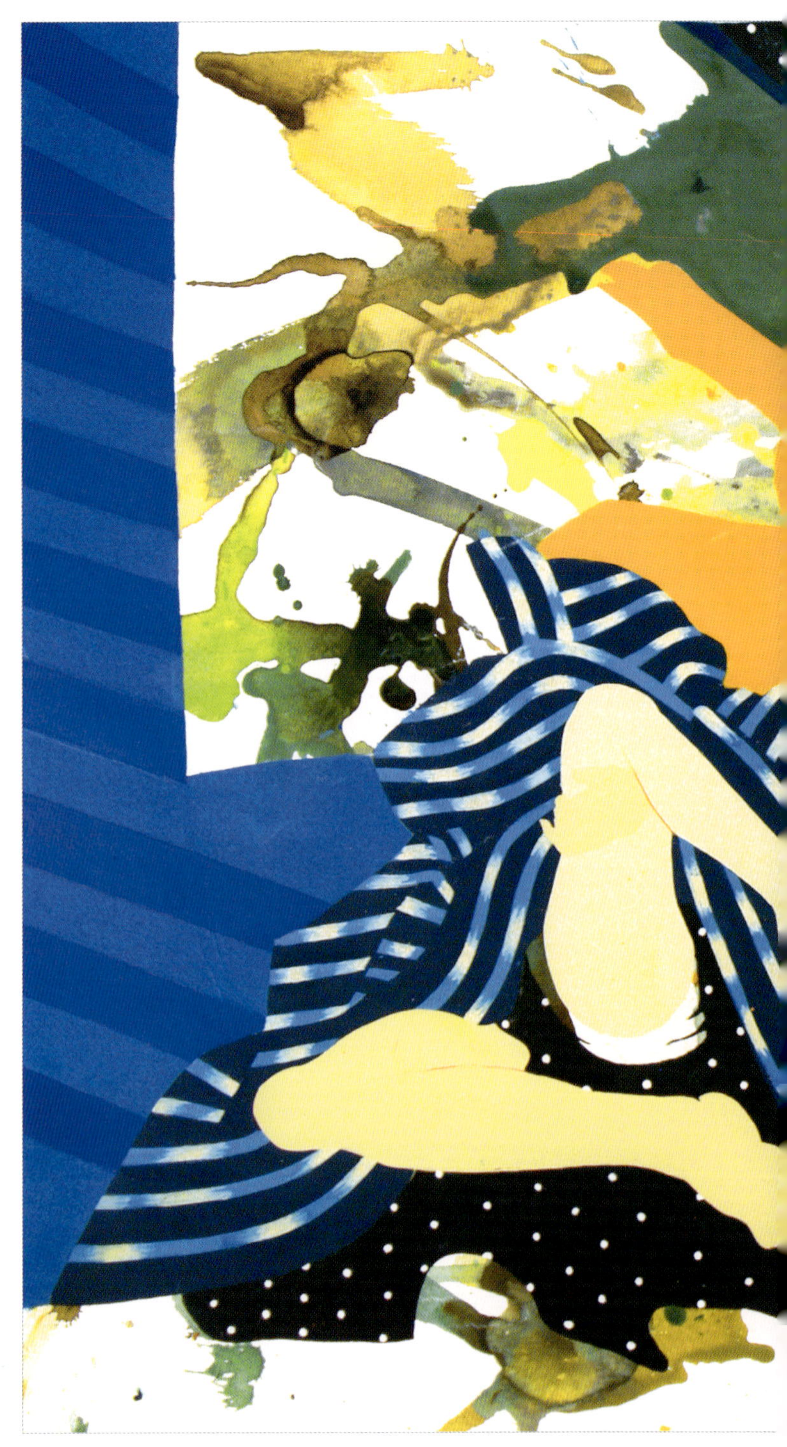

Shunger, 2006
Acrylic on paper
20 x 29"

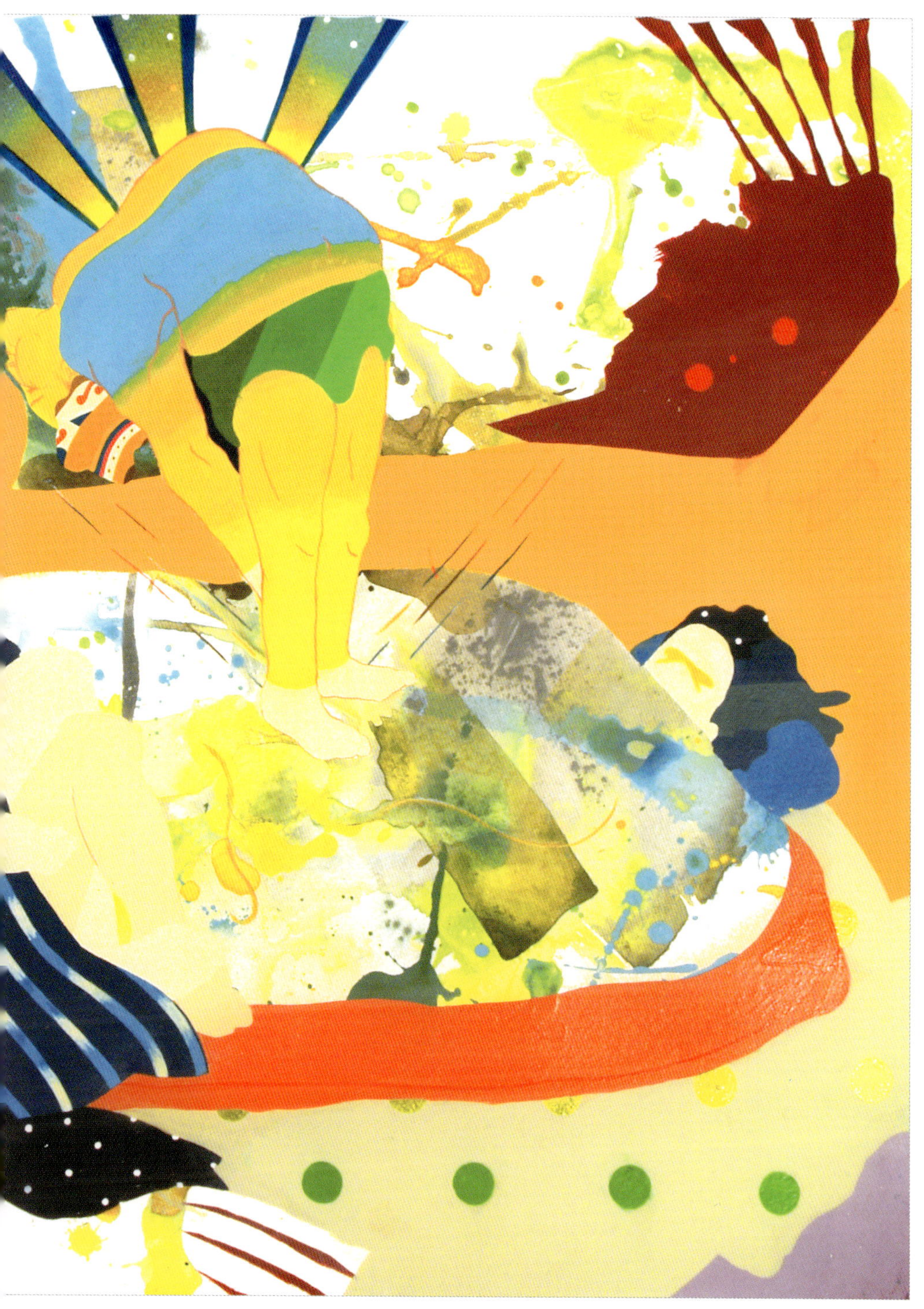

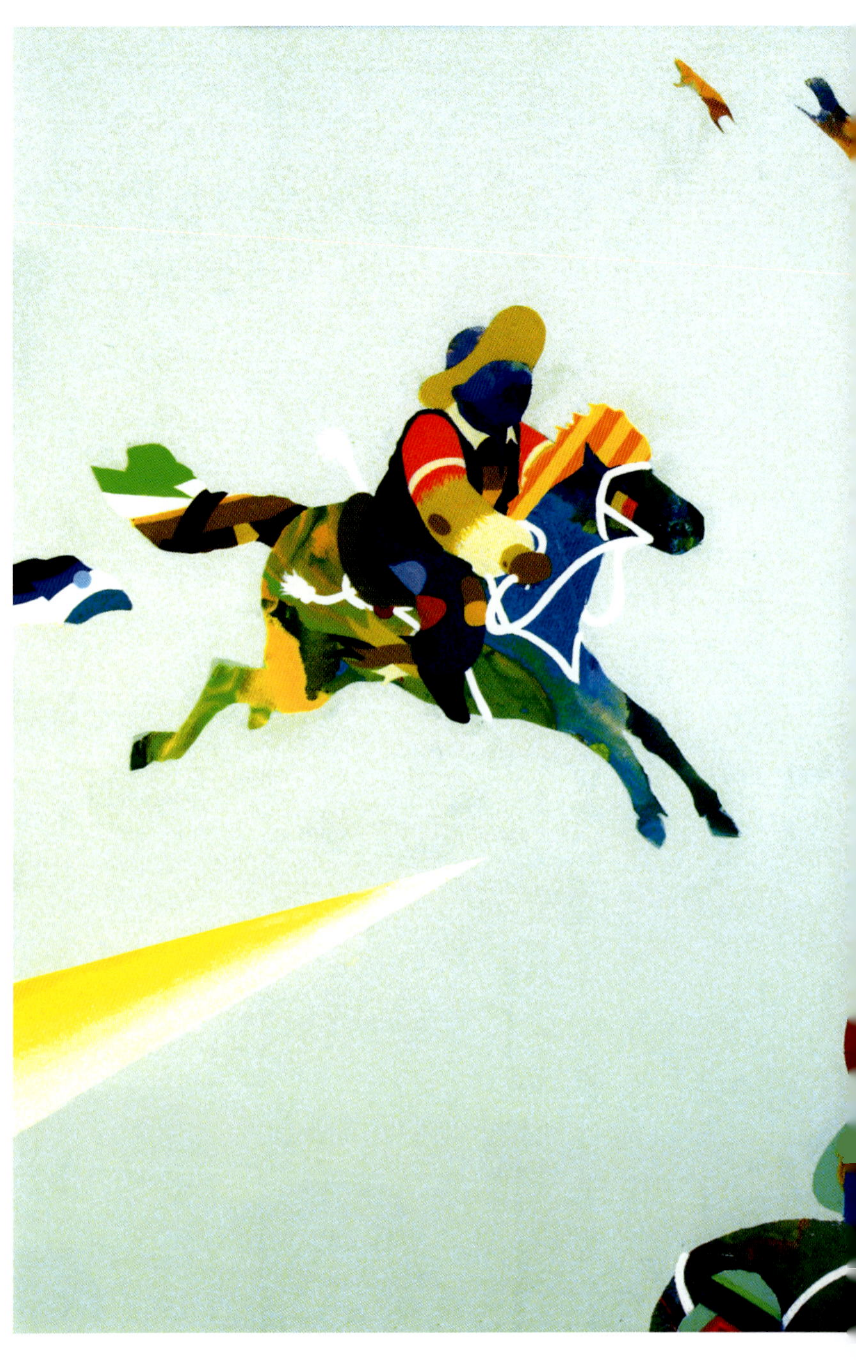

3rip-Horse, 2006
Acrylic on canvas
24 x 36"

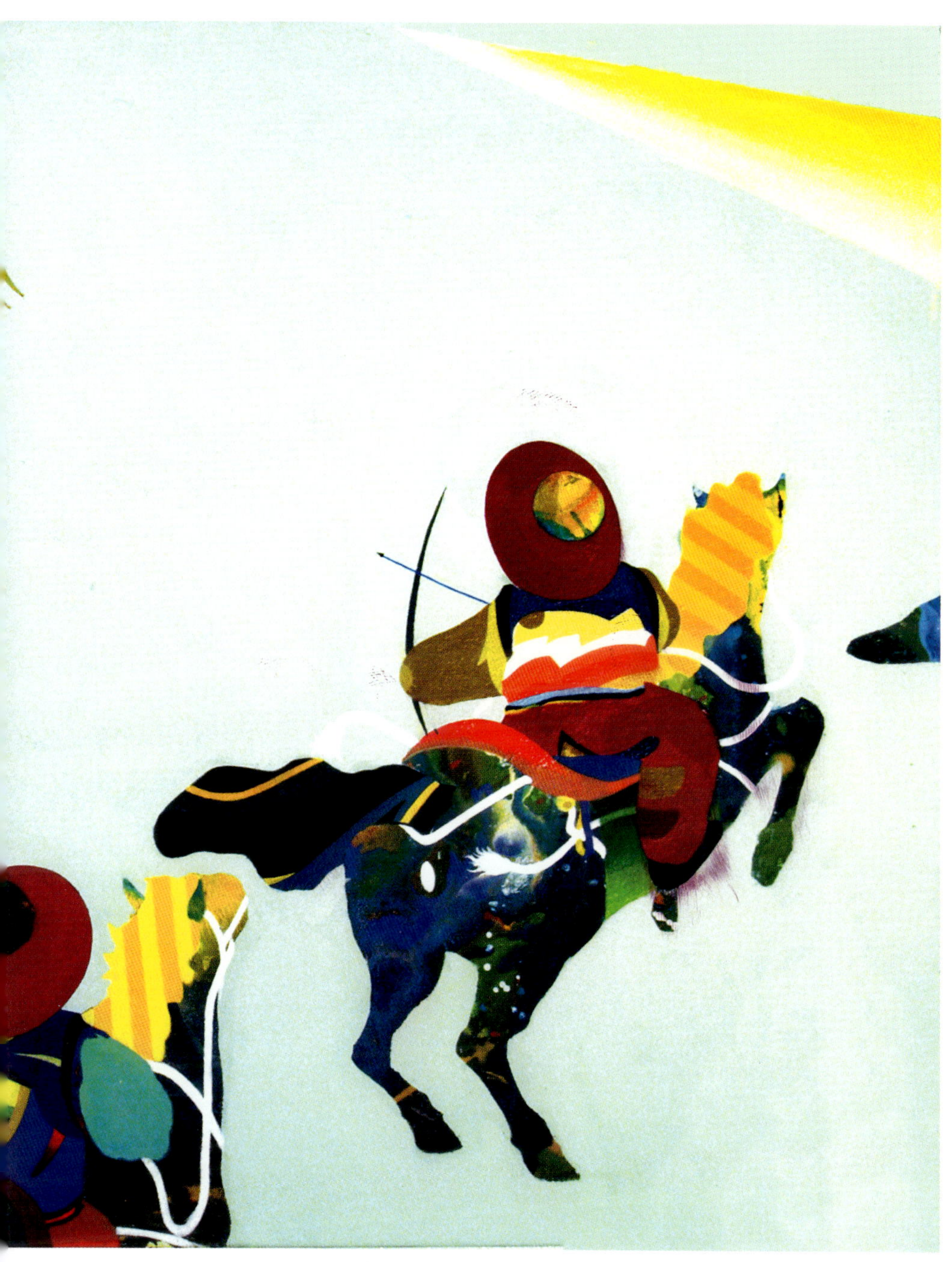

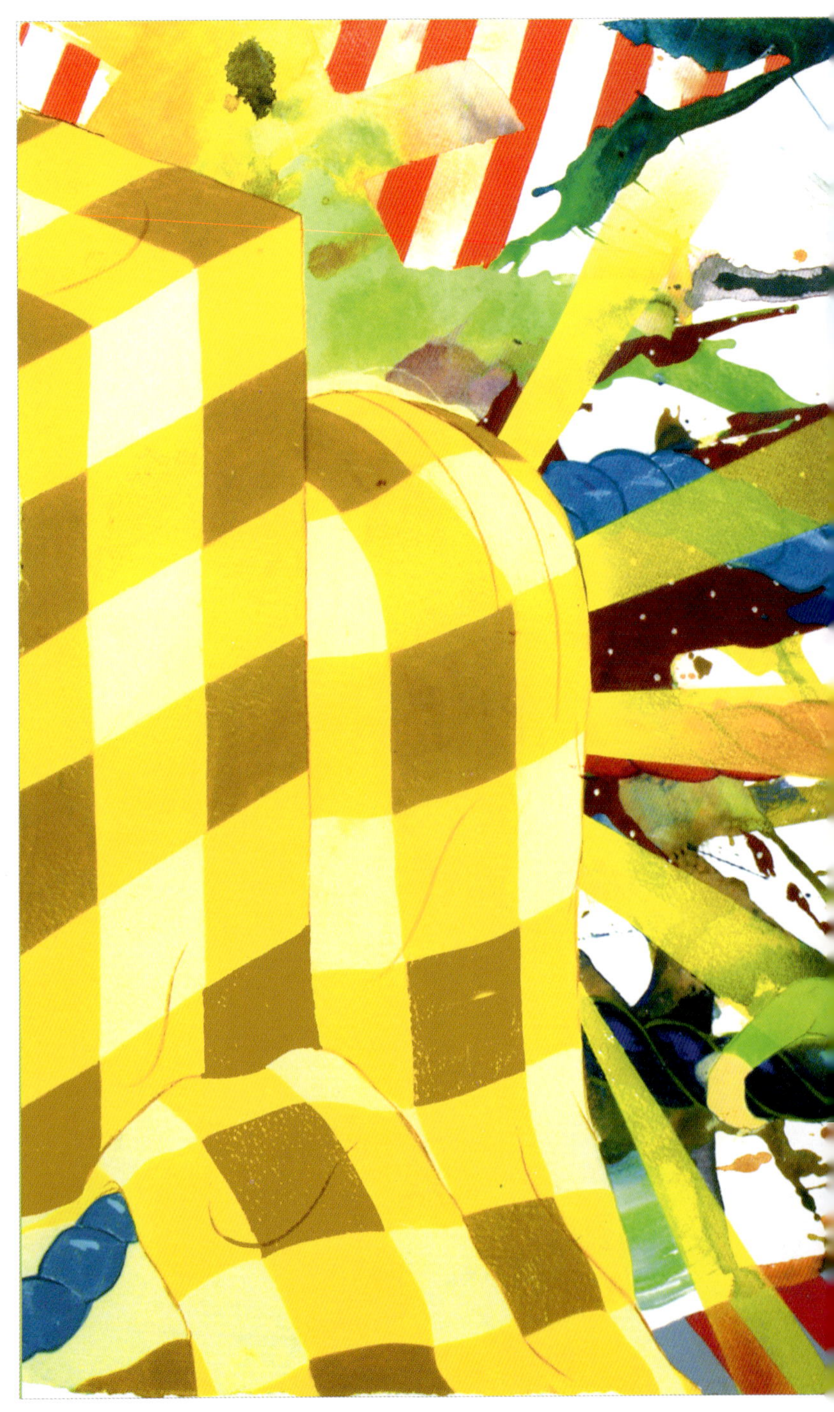

Day Dream, 2006
Acrylic on paper
20 x 29"

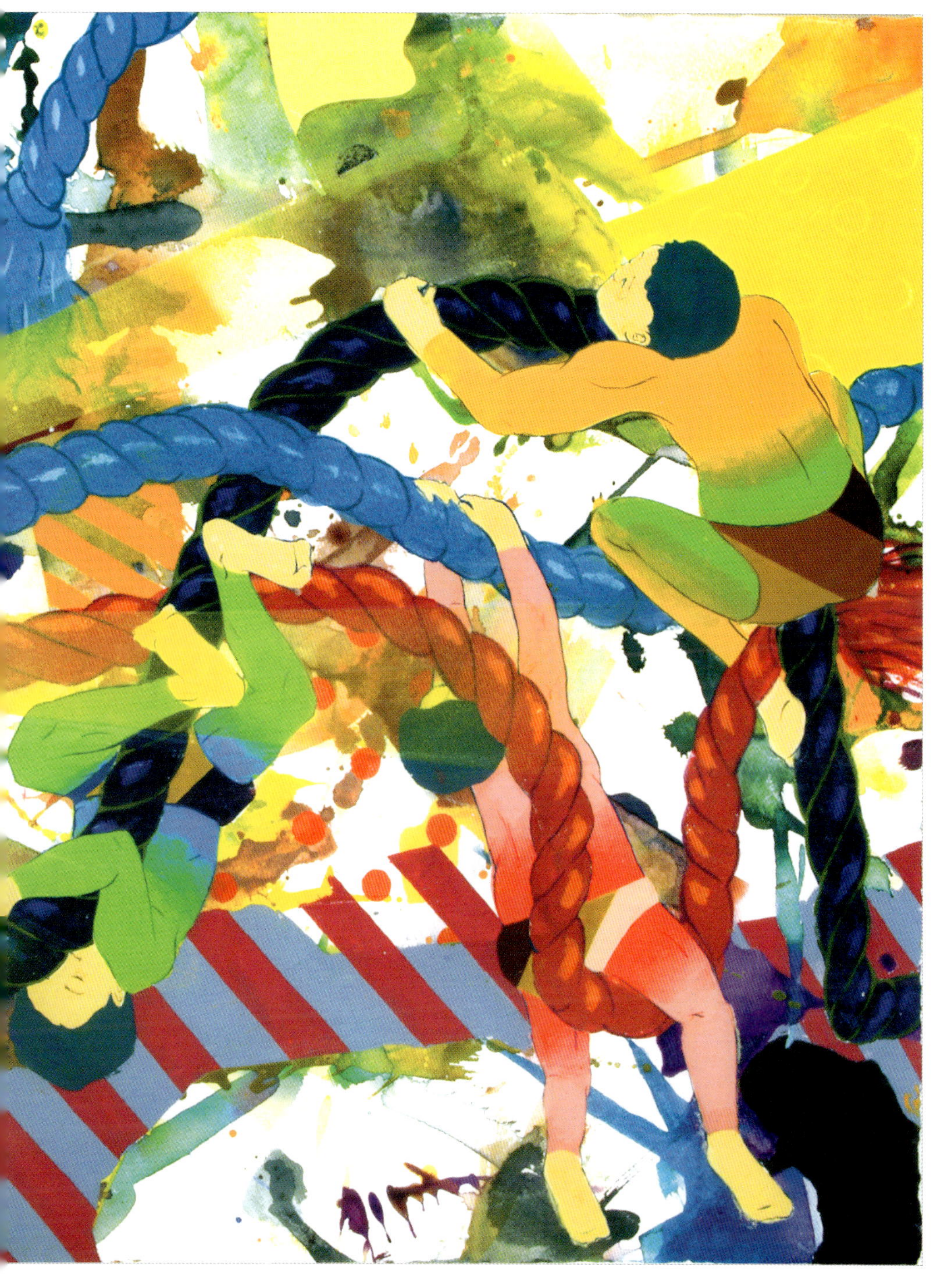

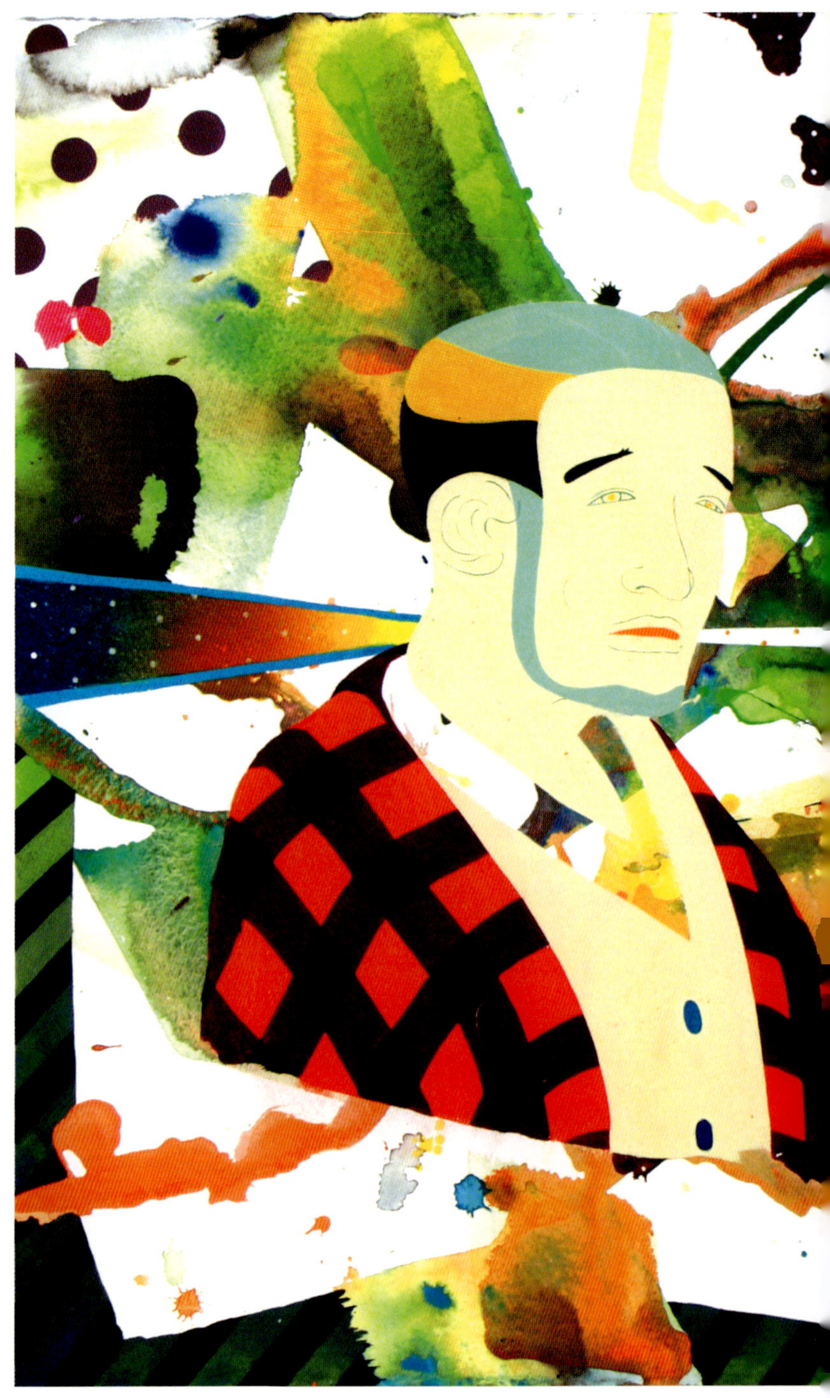

Yarkshaw, 2006
Acrylic on paper
20 x 28"

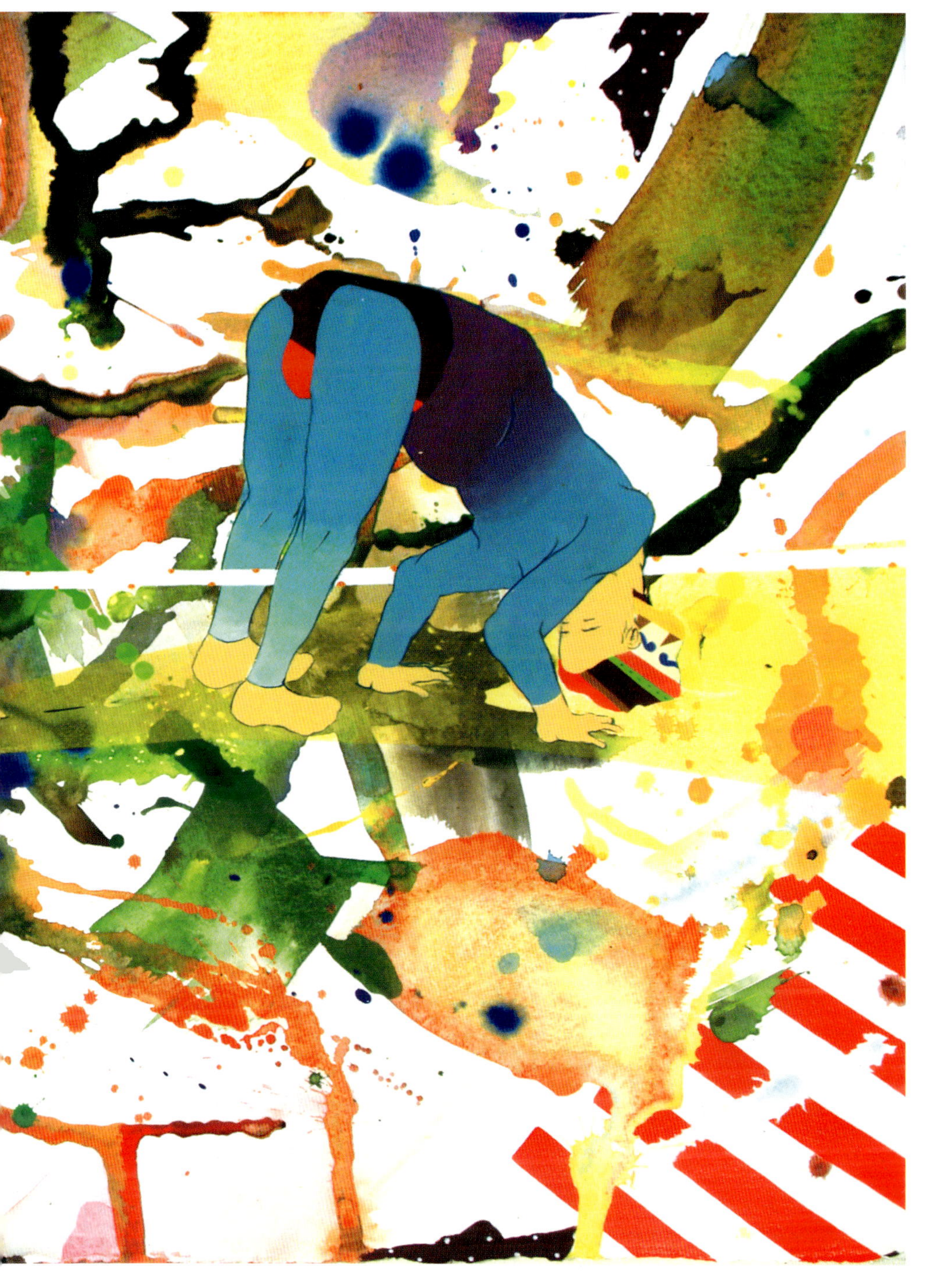

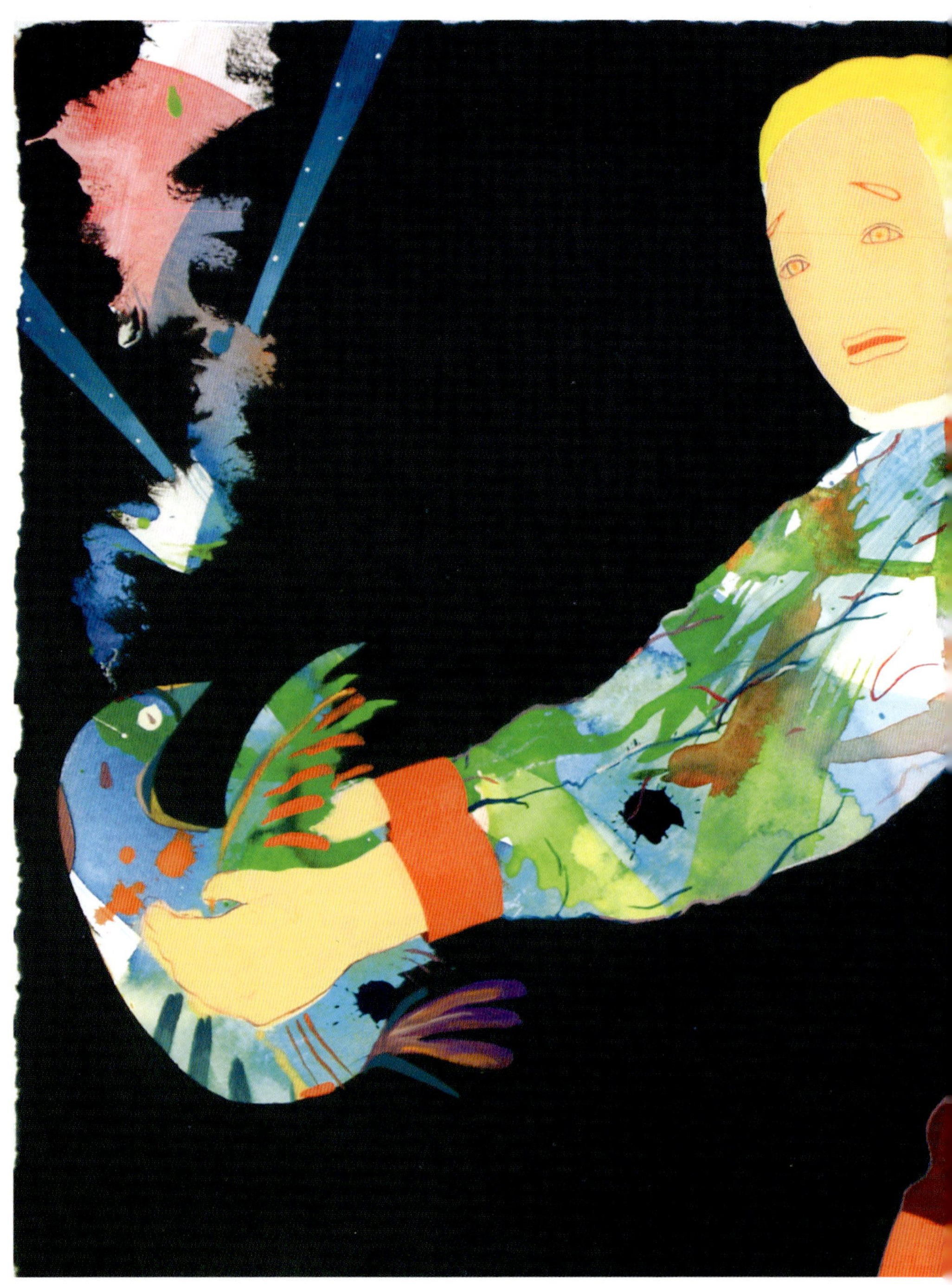

Release, 2006
Acrylic on paper
15 x 23"

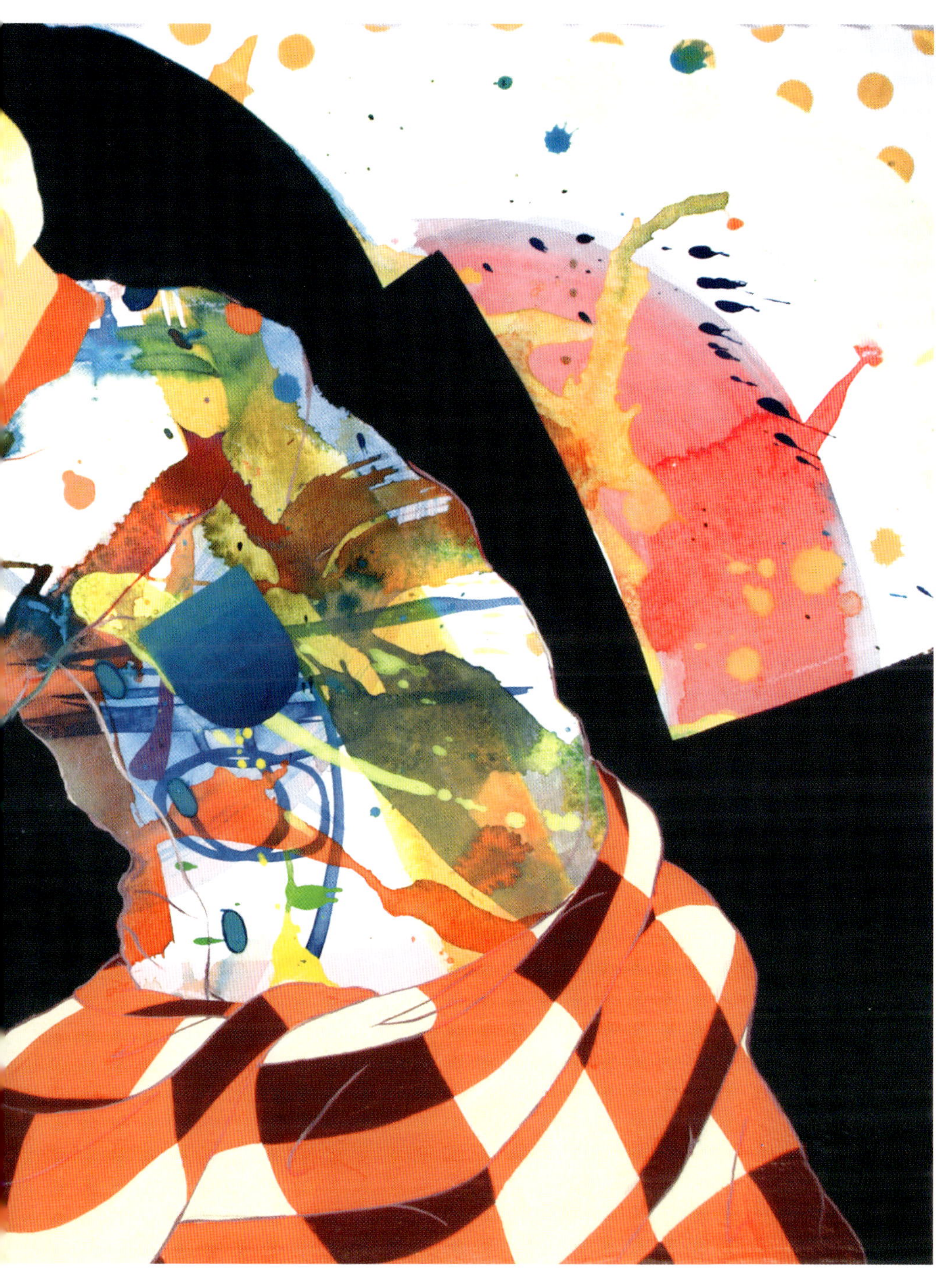

Summer-Talk, 2006
Acrylic on paper
20 x 29"

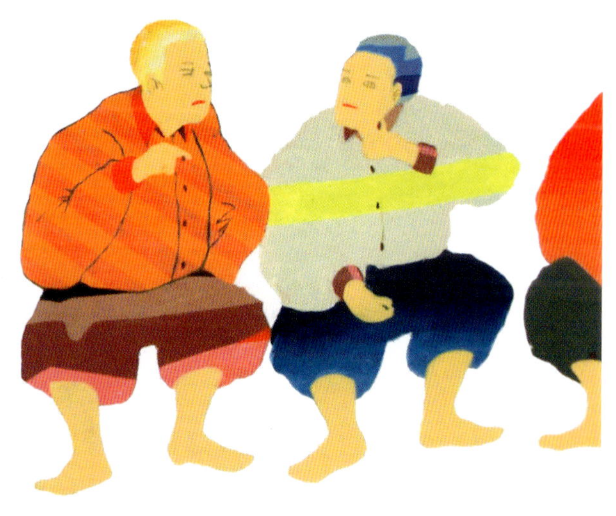

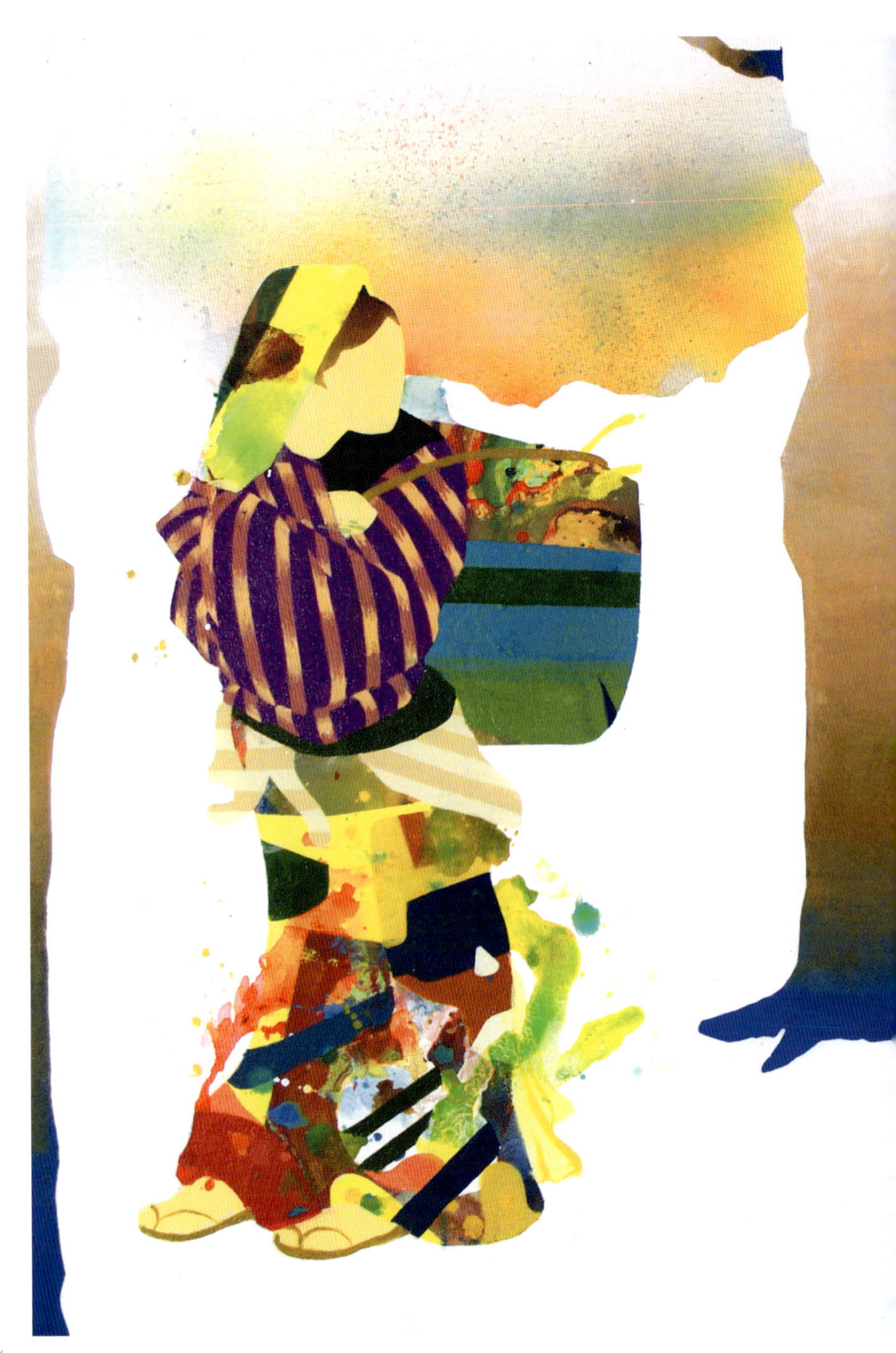

Ladiy, 2006
Acrylic on canvas
24 x 36"

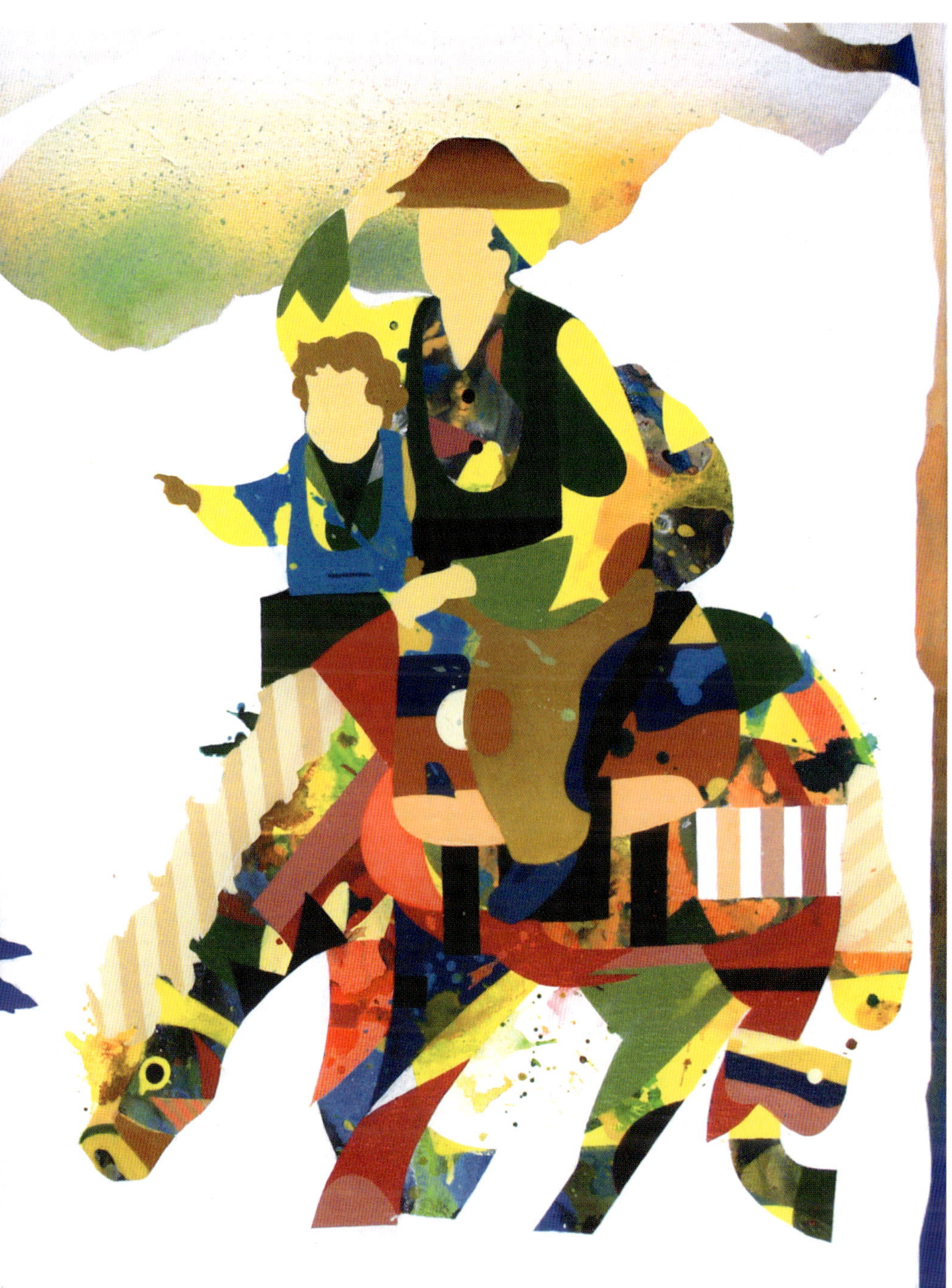

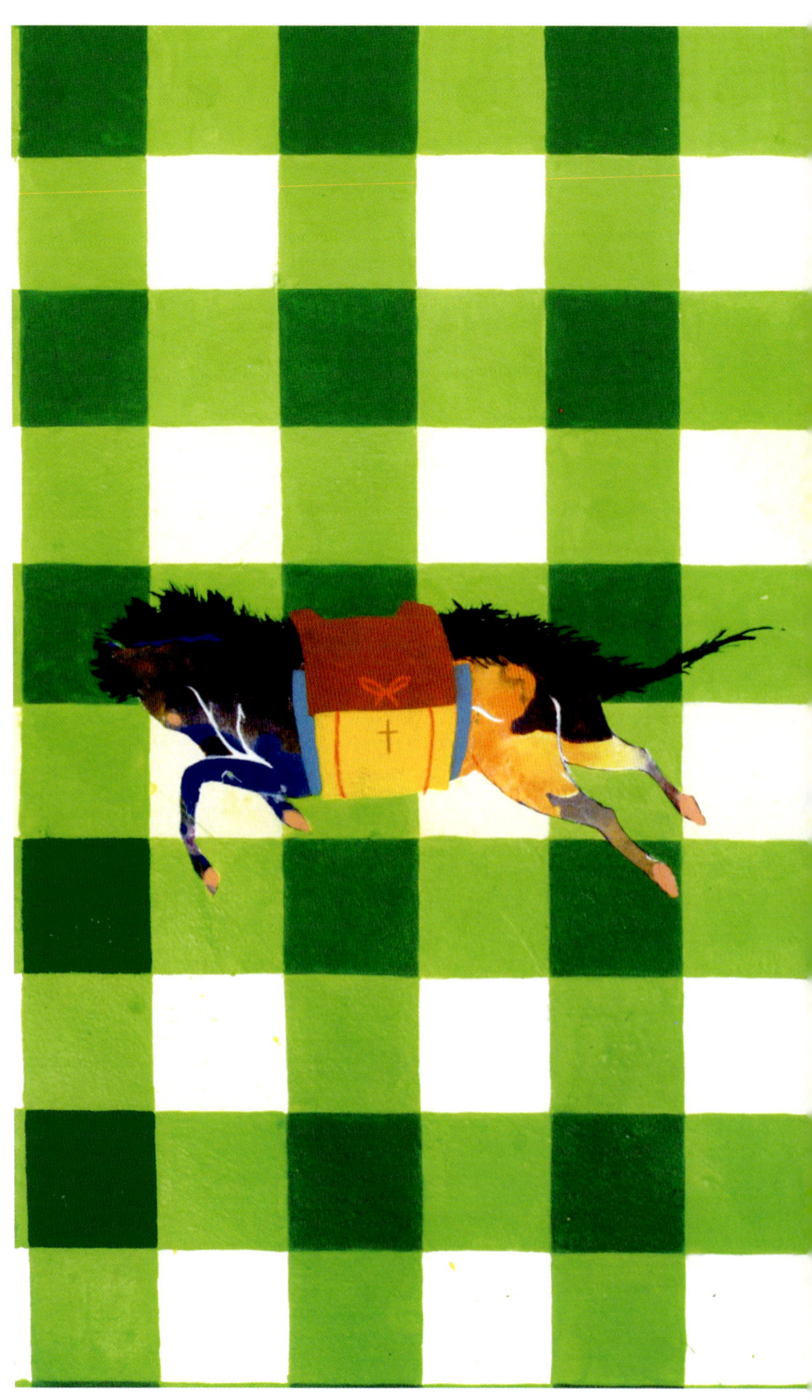

Crypto-Christian, 2006
Acrylic on paper
20 x 29"

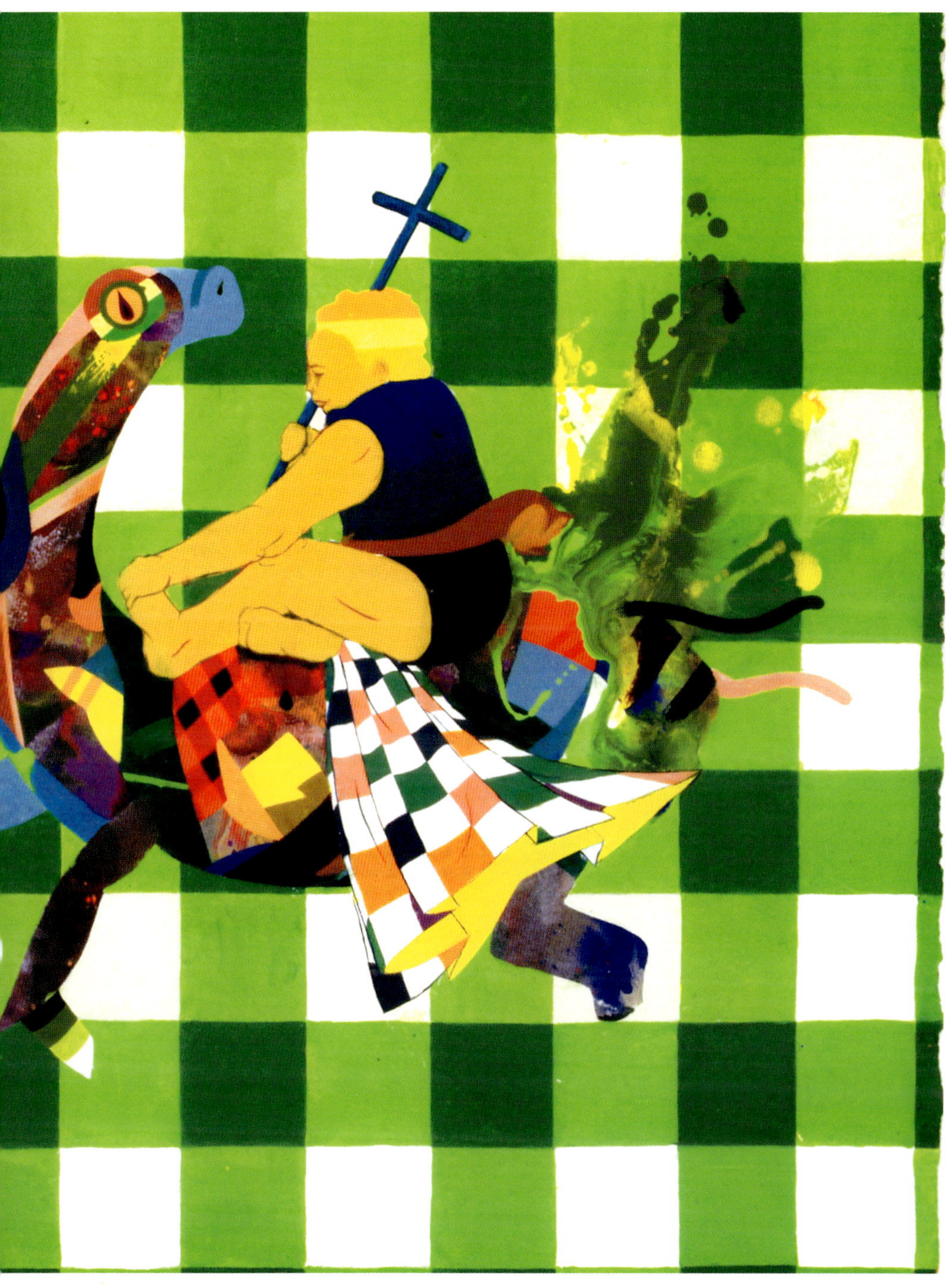

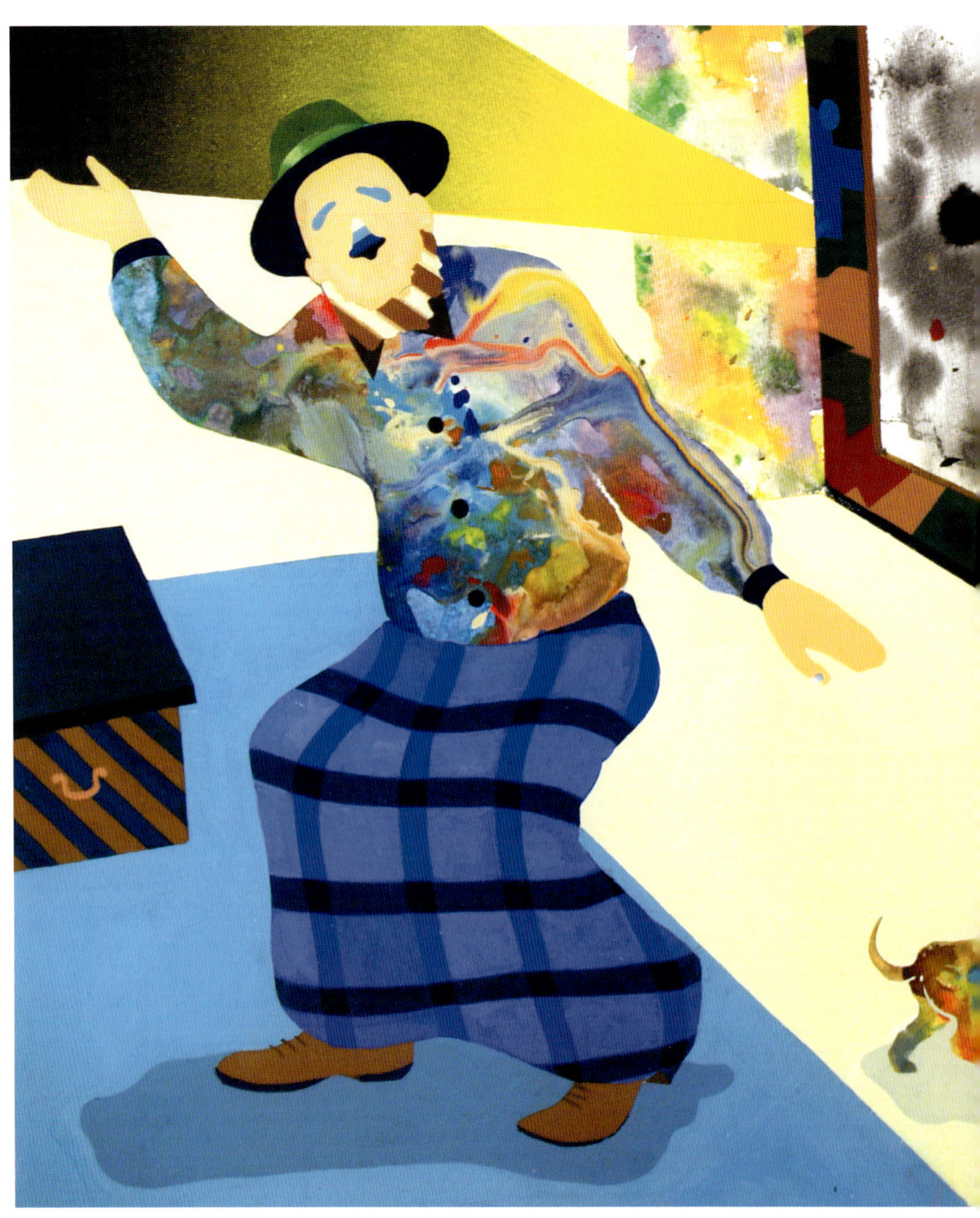

Unit, 2006
Acrylic on paper
18 x 32"

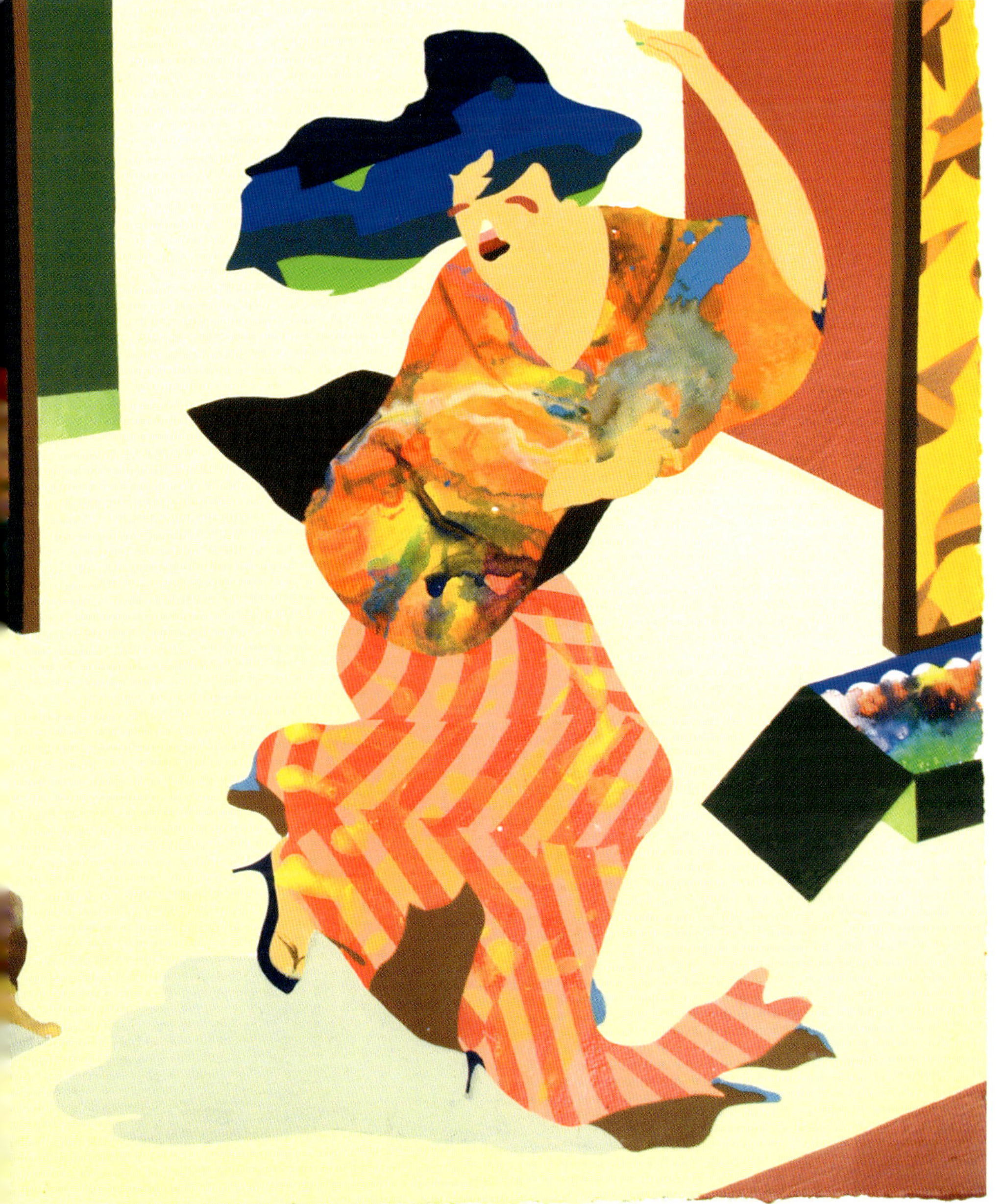

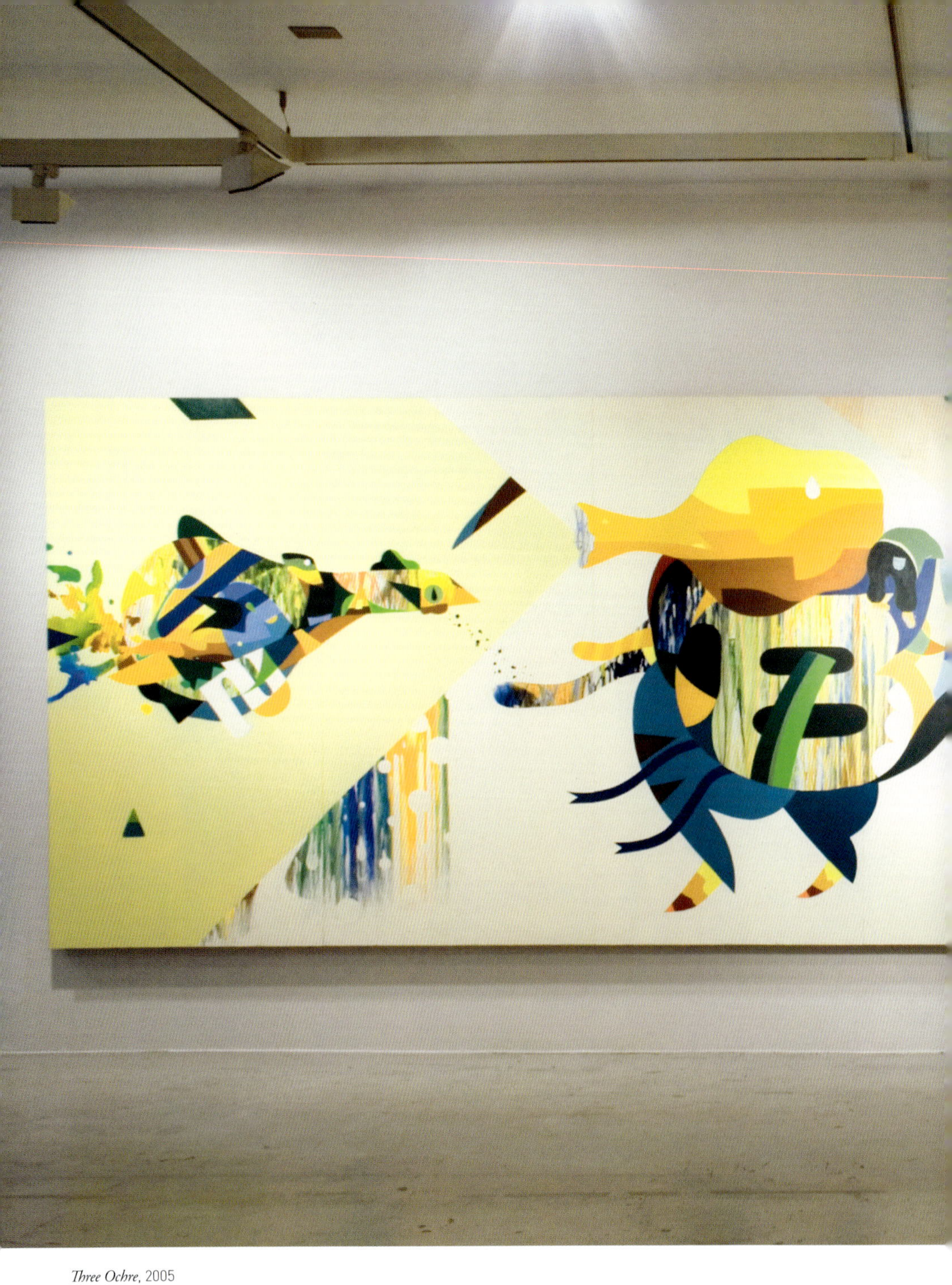

Three Ochre, 2005
Acrylic on wood panel
87 x 275 x 2.5"

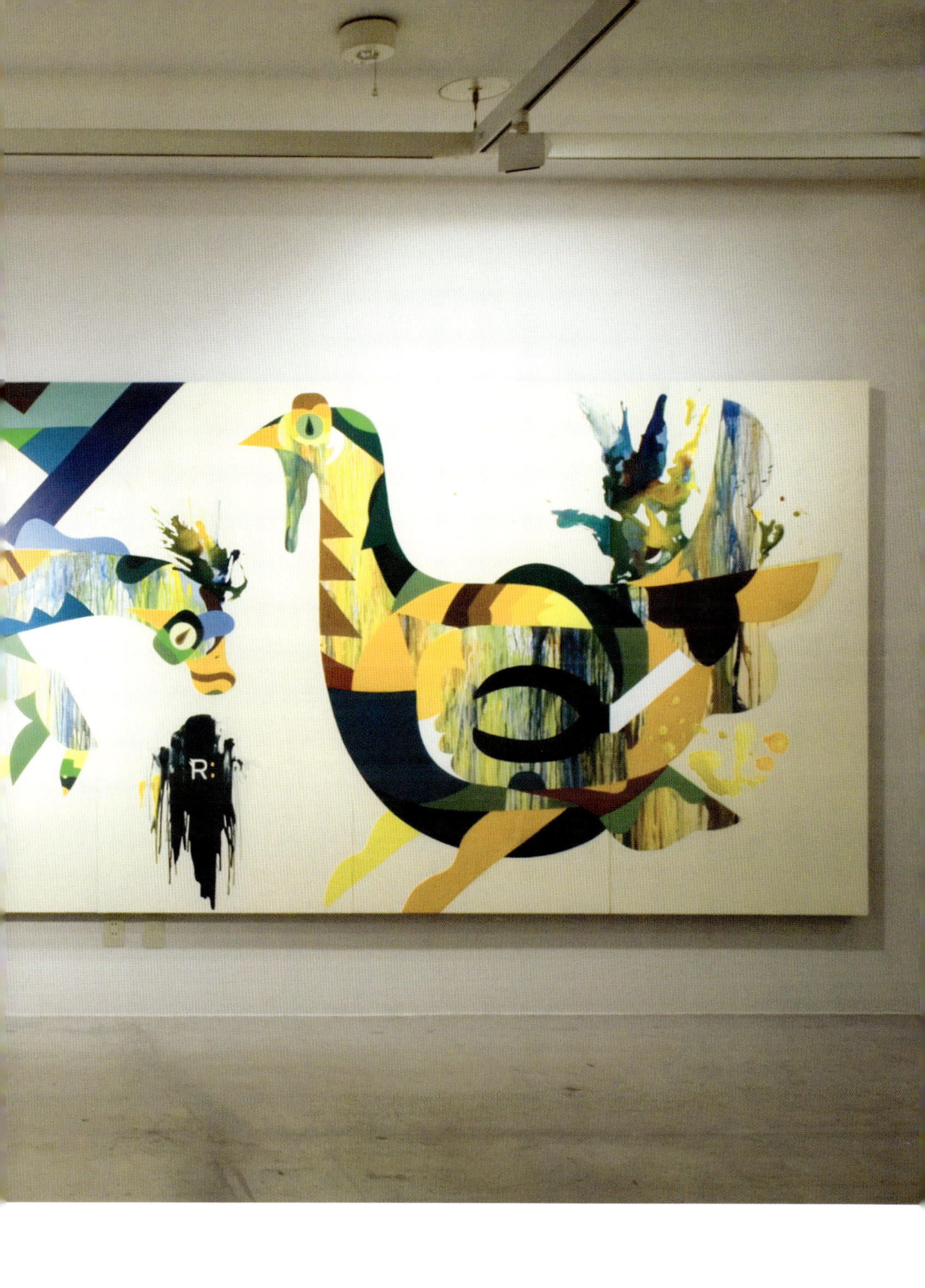
R:

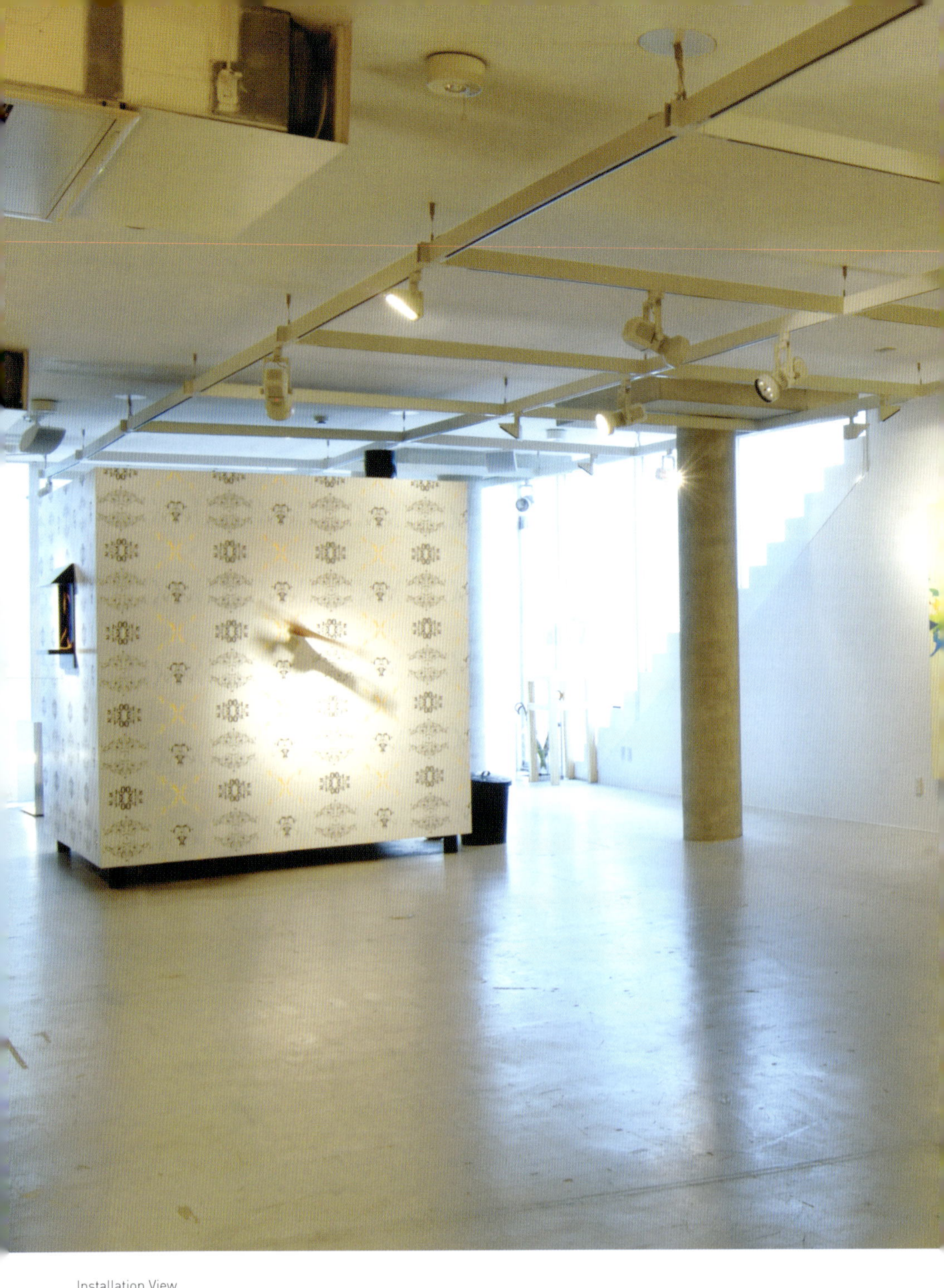

Installation View
Gallery Speak For, Tokyo, 2006

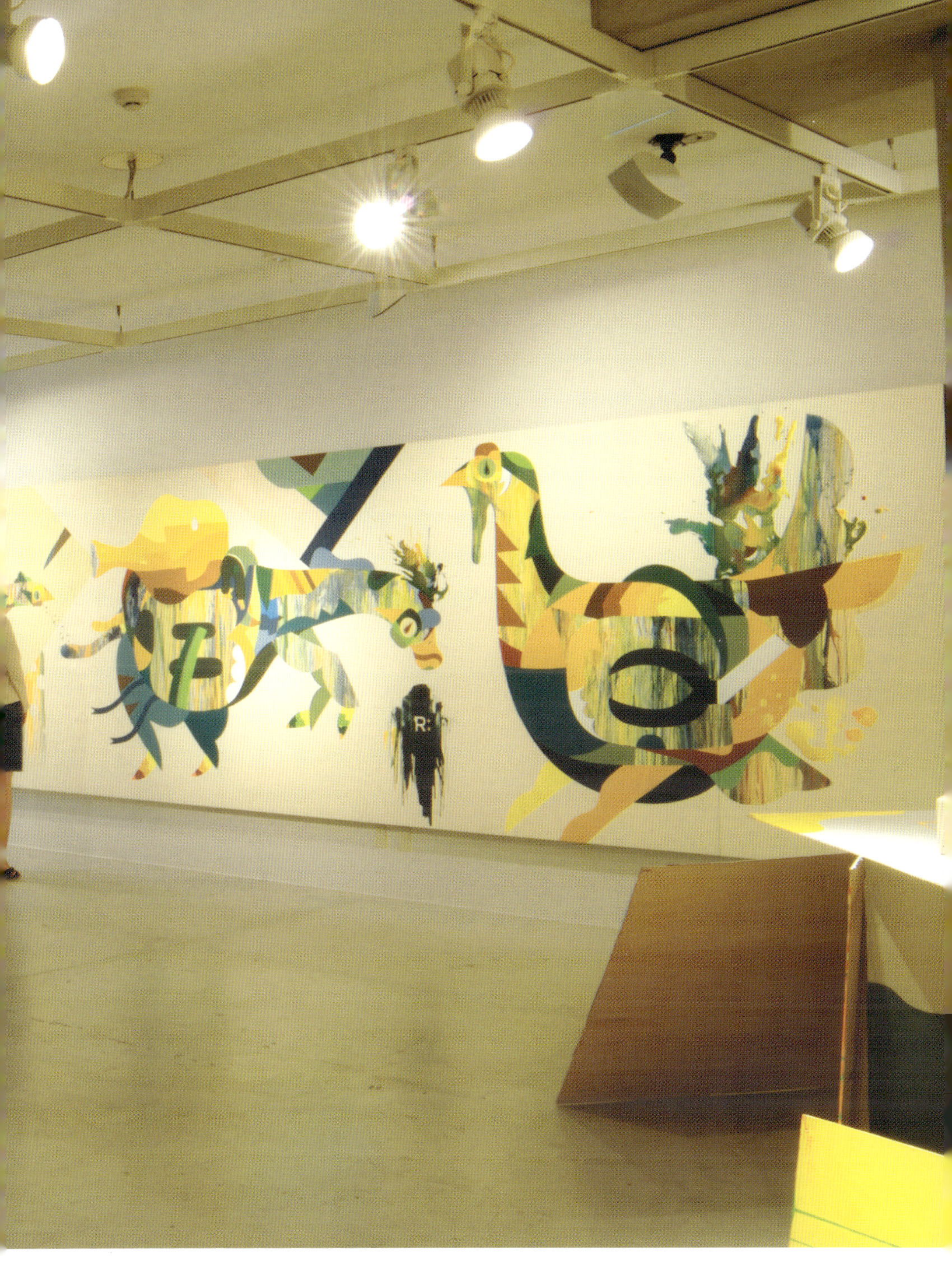
R:

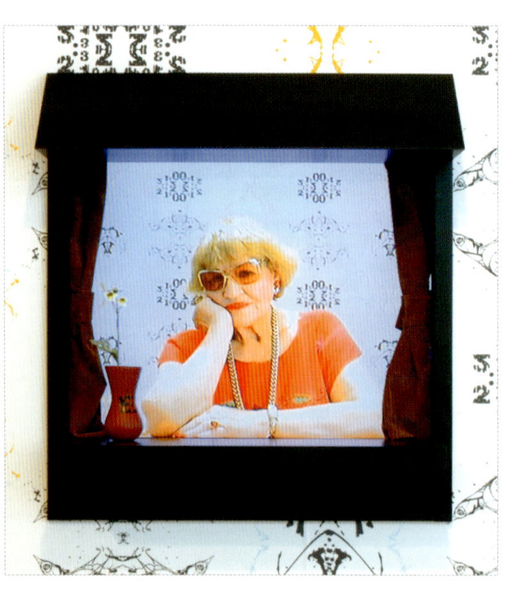

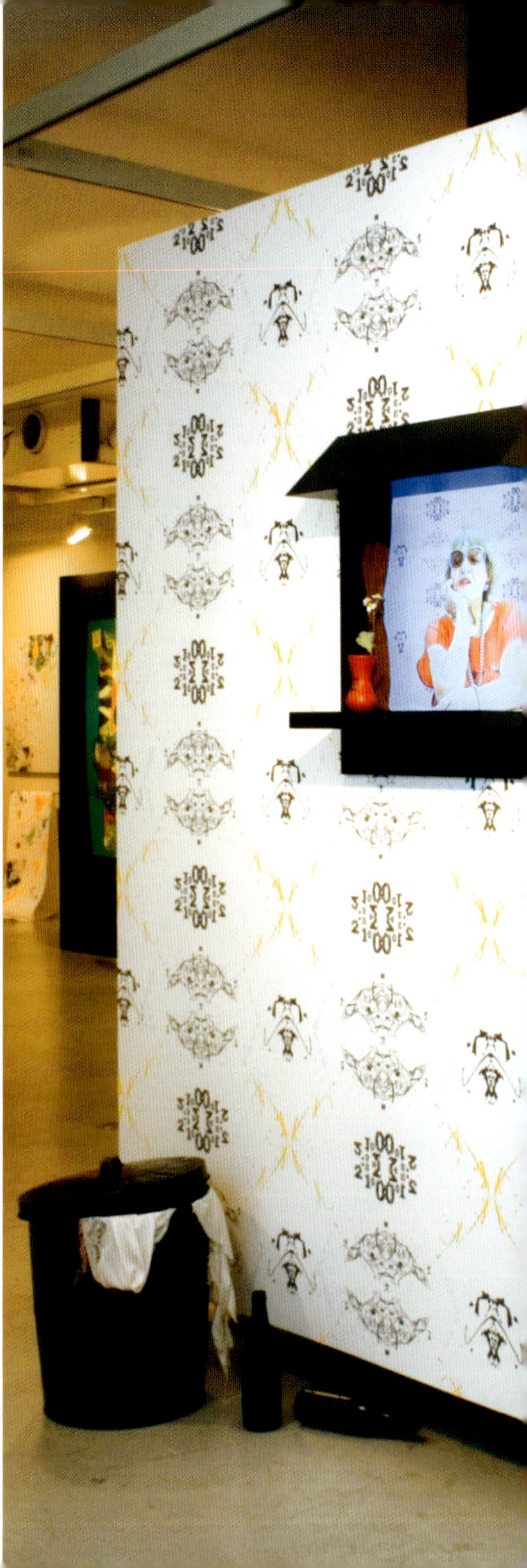

Leonora Music Vox, 2006
29" TV monitor, DVD player, silk screen wallpaper, wood, metal, glass, electric motor, acrylic on paper
87 x 87 x 98"

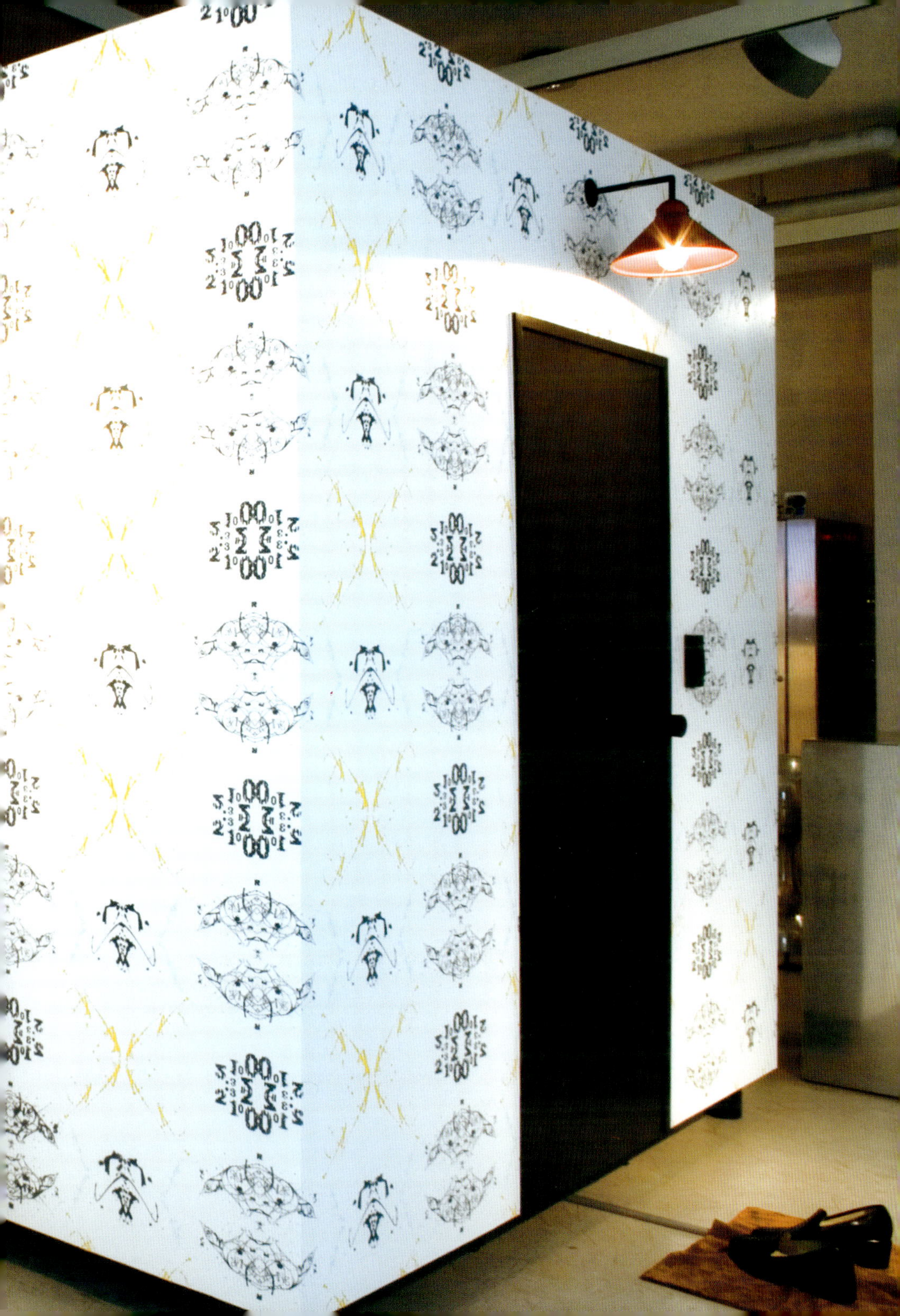

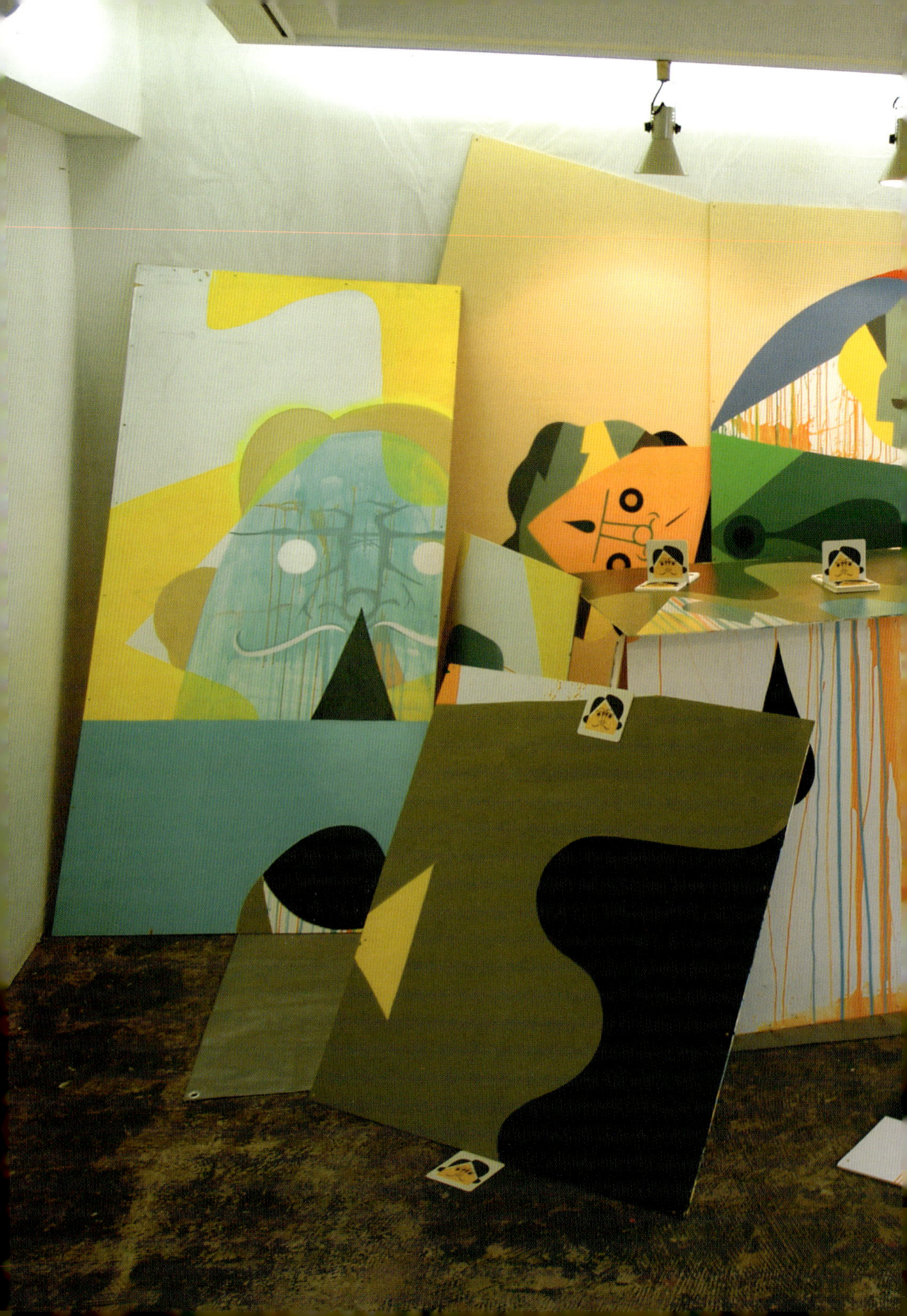

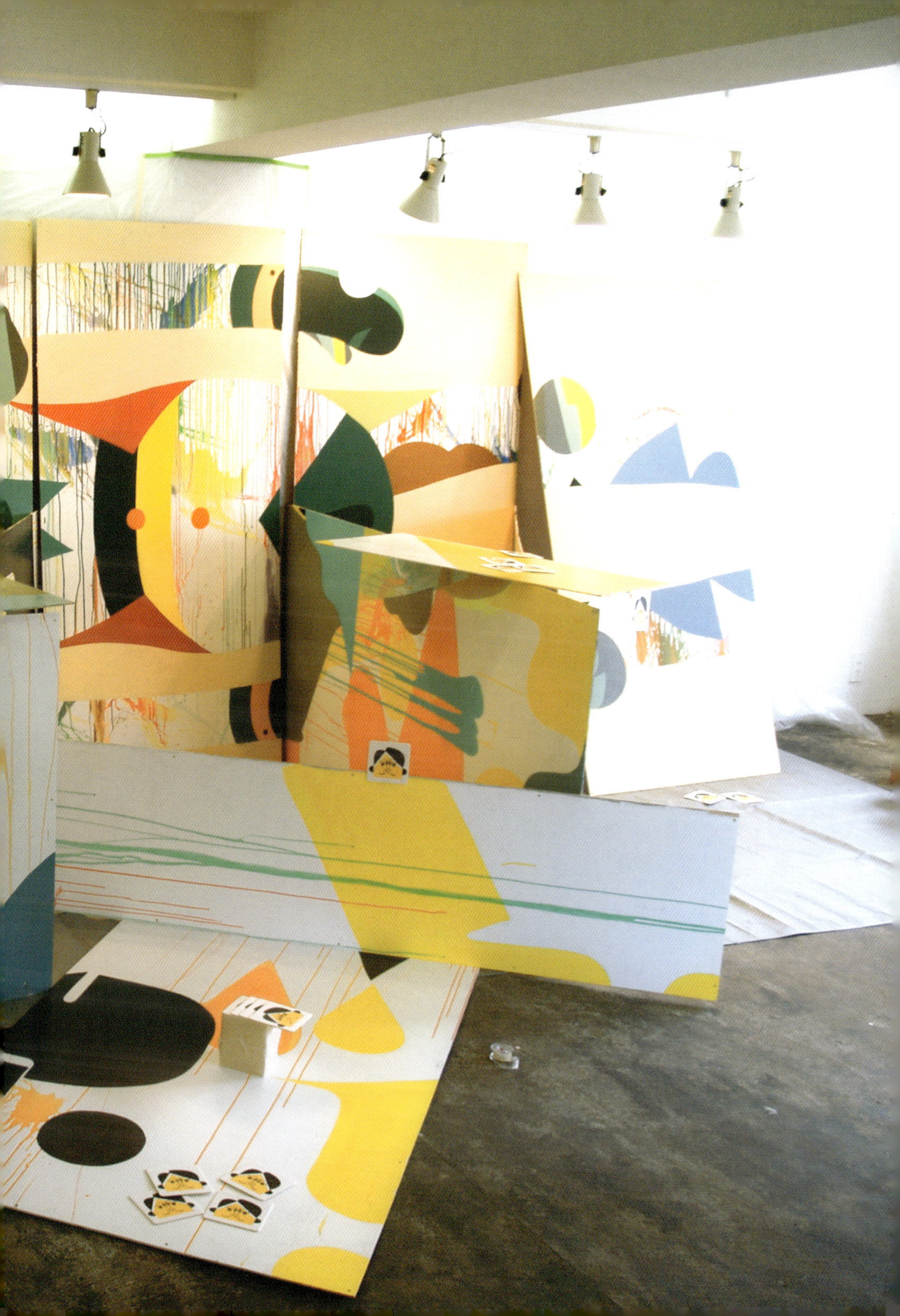

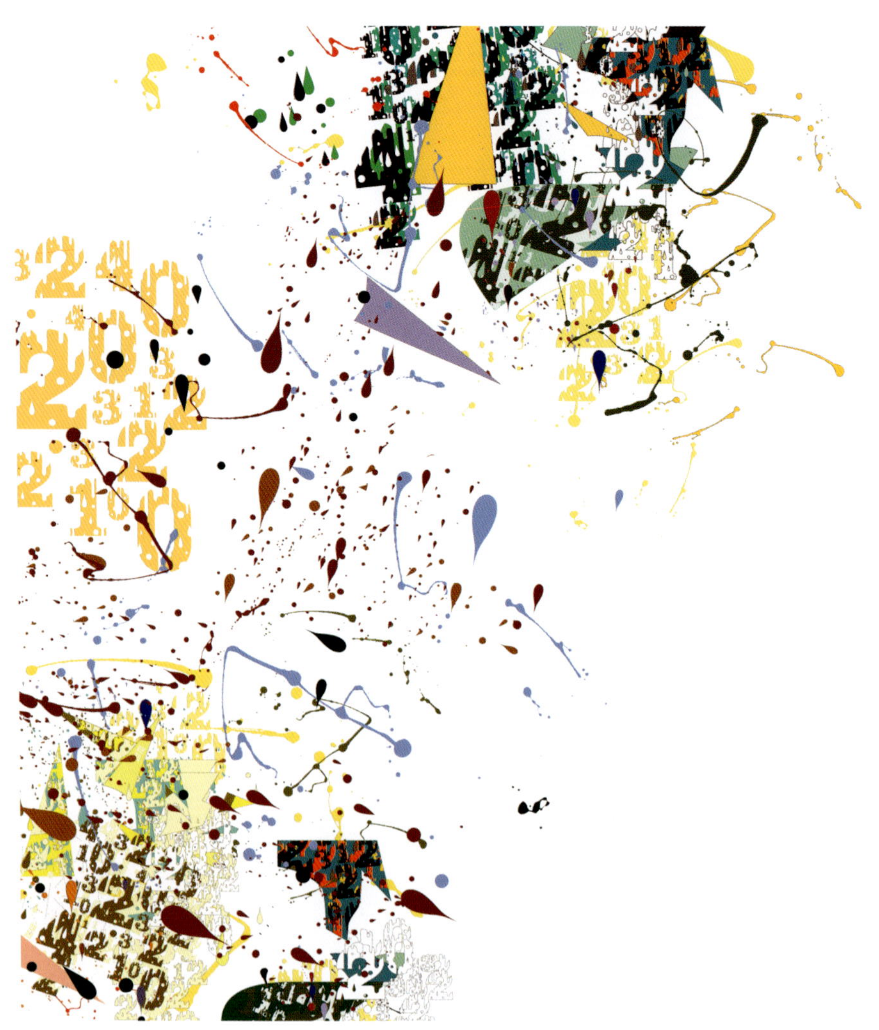

(previous page)
N•I•P, 2006
Acrylic on wood panel, CD sound system,
speaker, silk screen on paper
80 x 240 x 100"

(right page and above)
Re-incarnation, 2006
Clear plexi-board, CMYK print, alluminum
60 x 30 x 24"

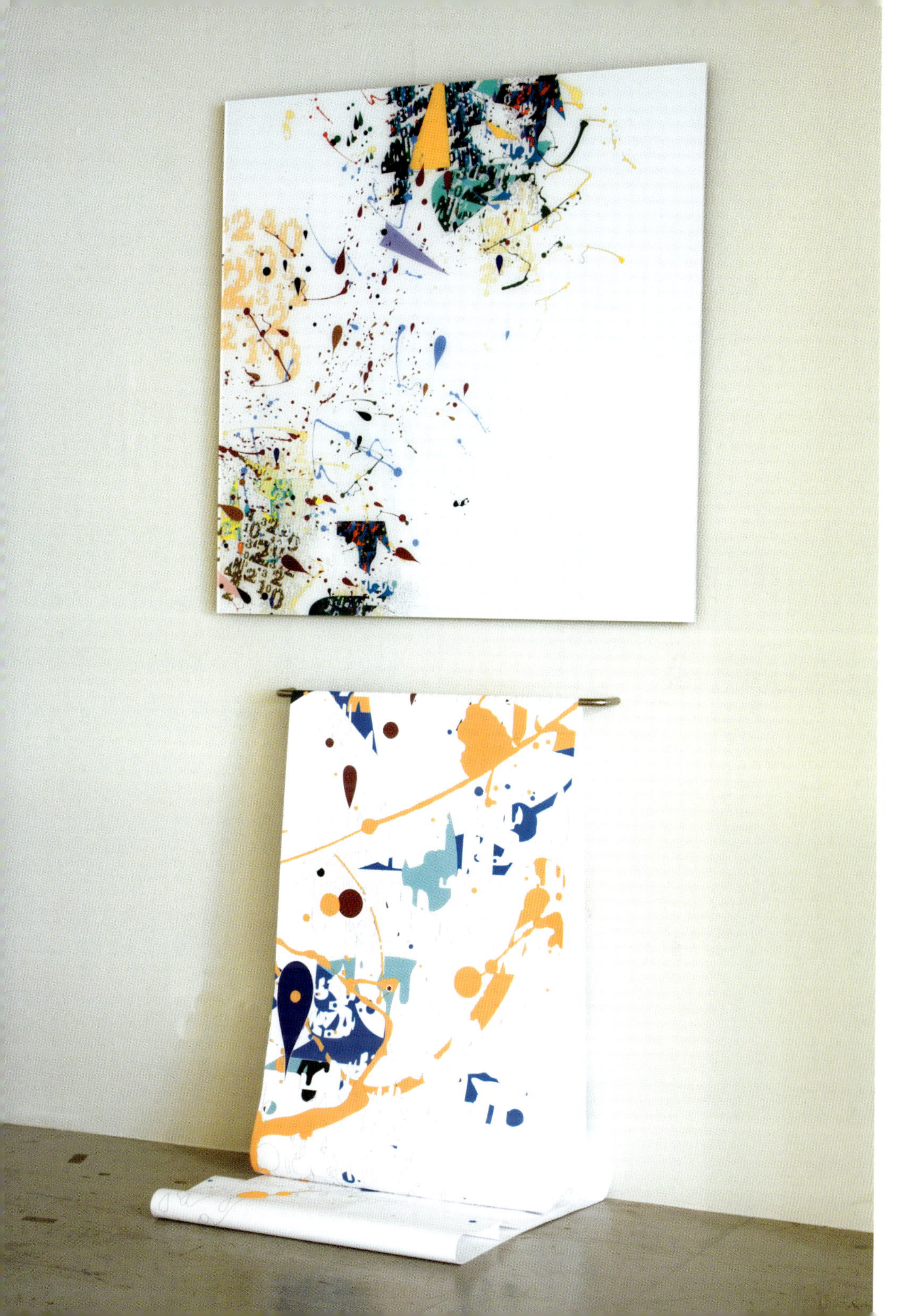

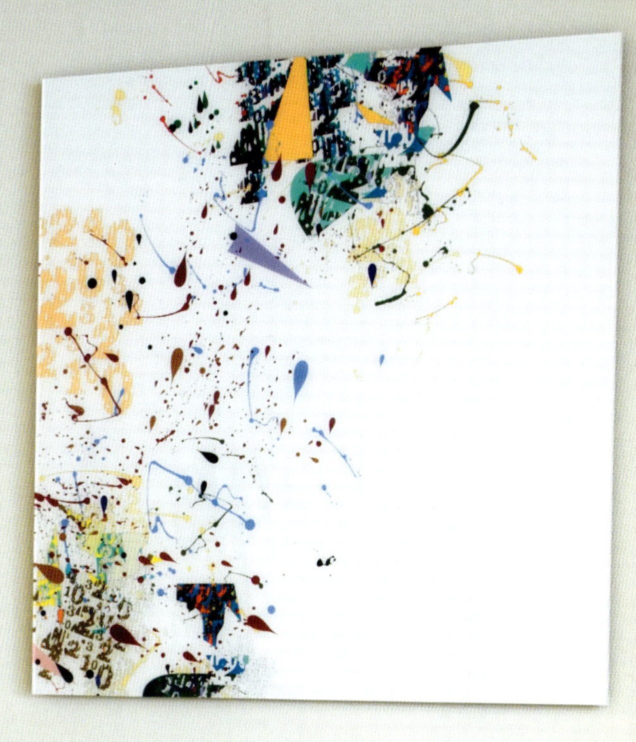

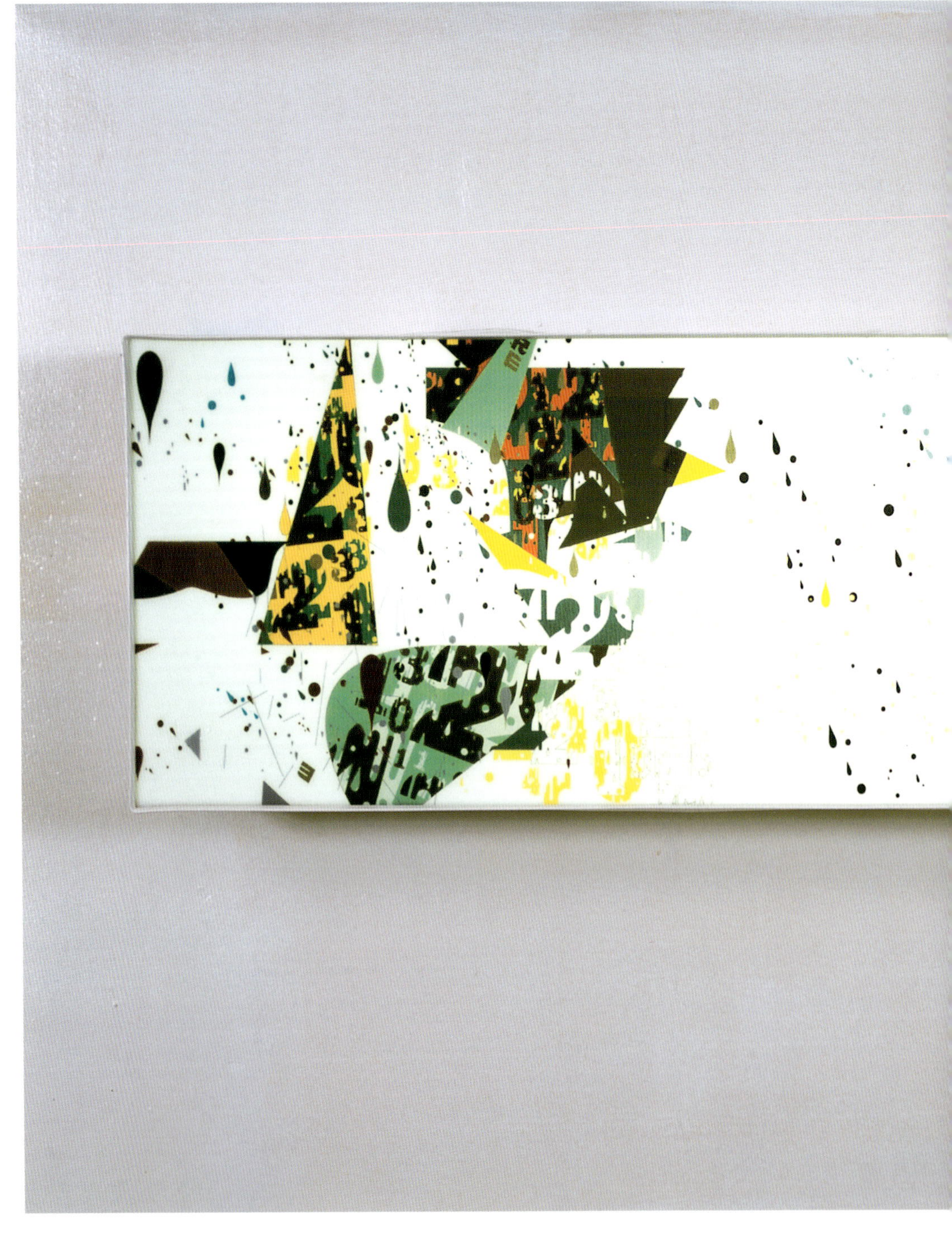

Re-incarnation, 2005
CMYK print, flourescent light, plastic, alluminum box
60 x 18 x 6"

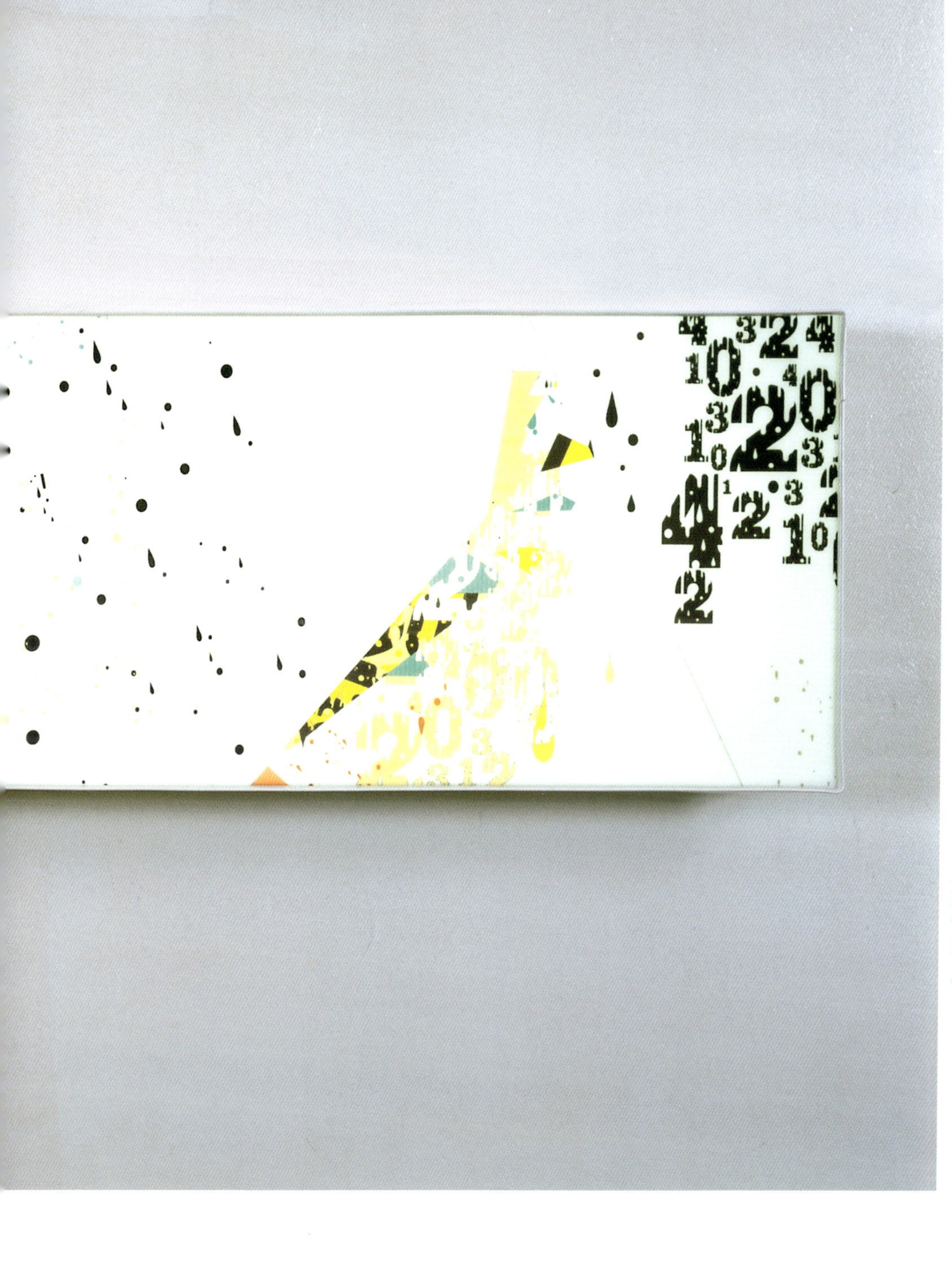

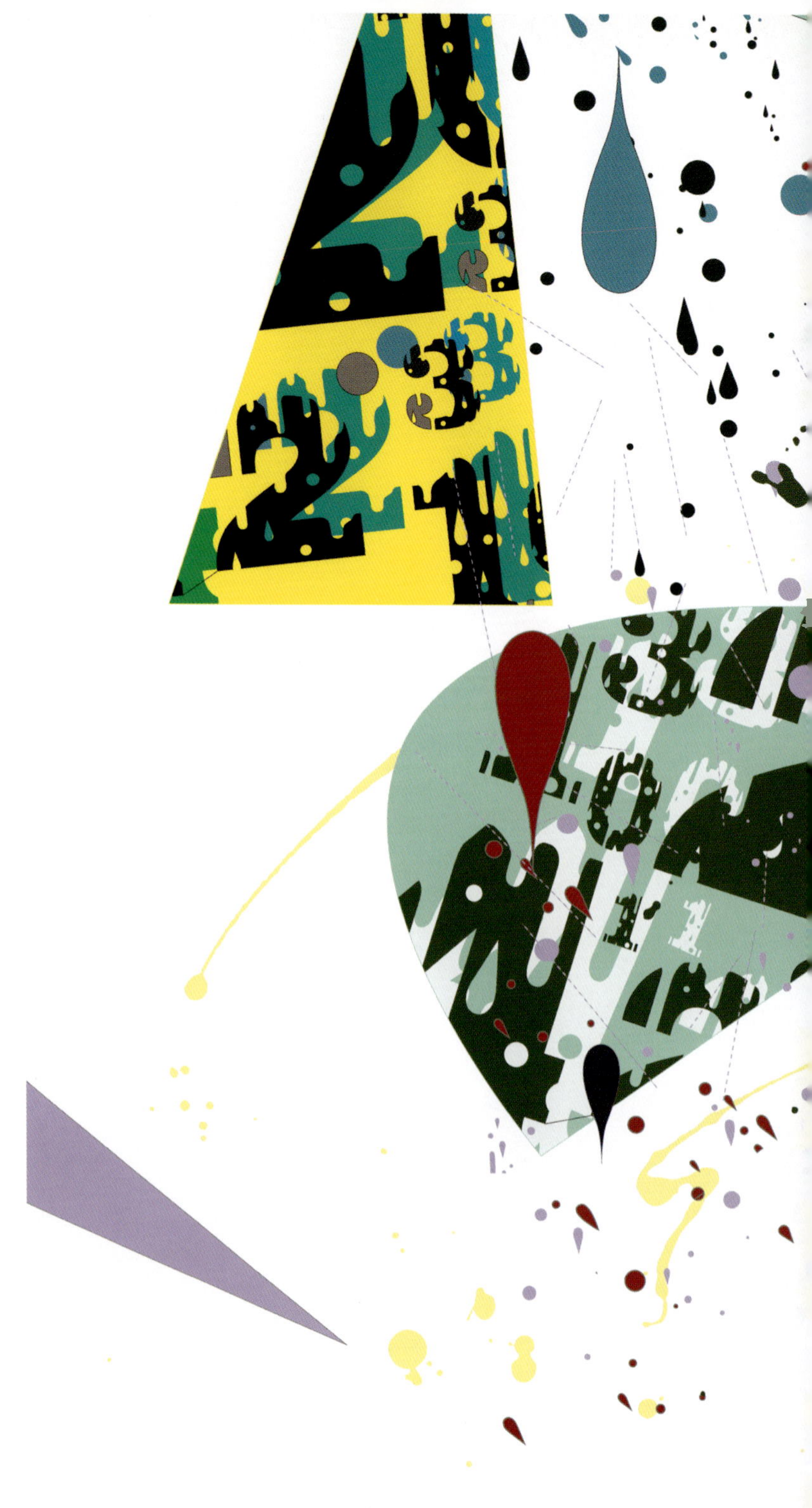

Re-incarnation, 2006
CMYK print
19 x 24"

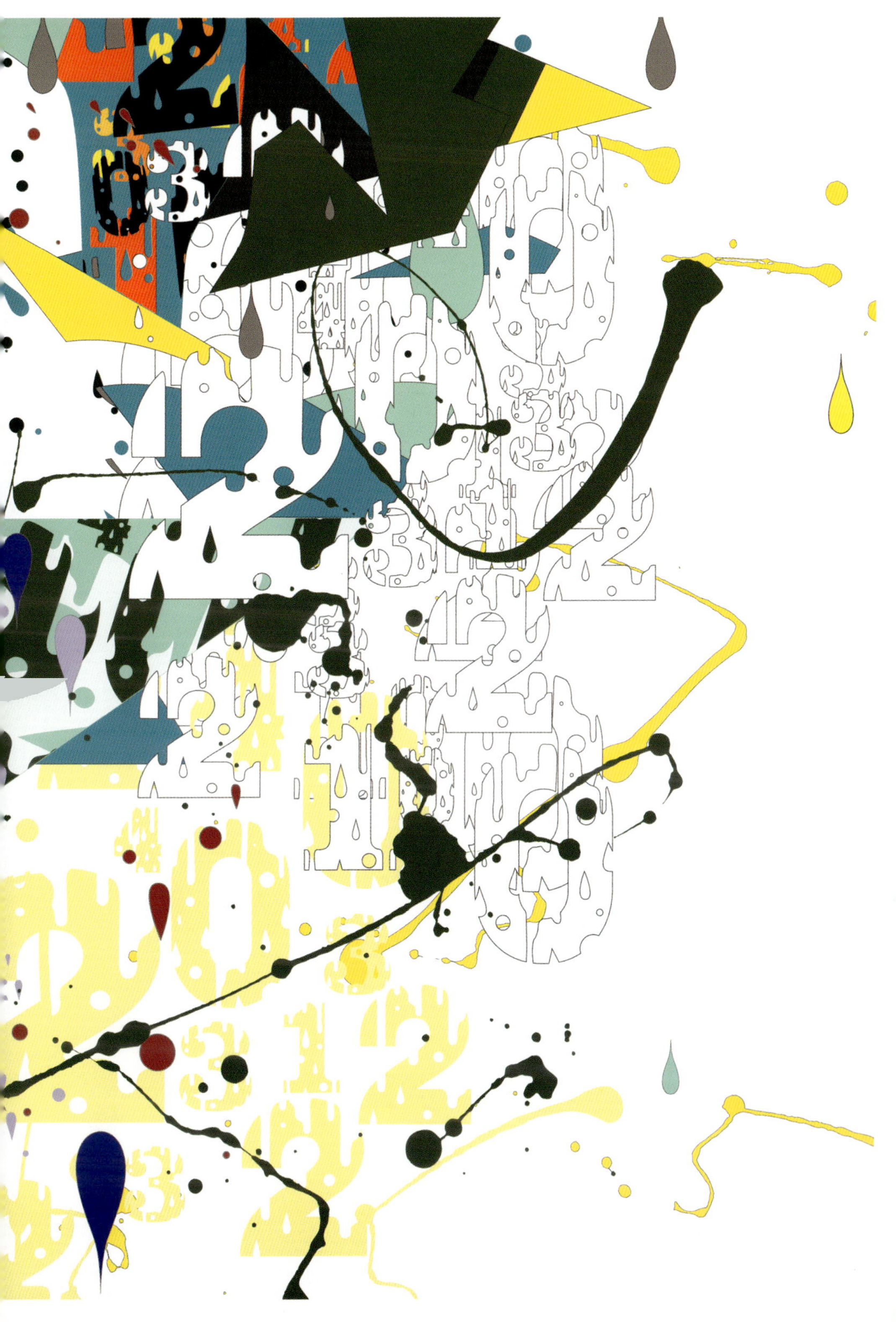

Drake/Swan, 2005
Acrylic on paper, silk screen wallpaper
58 x 28"

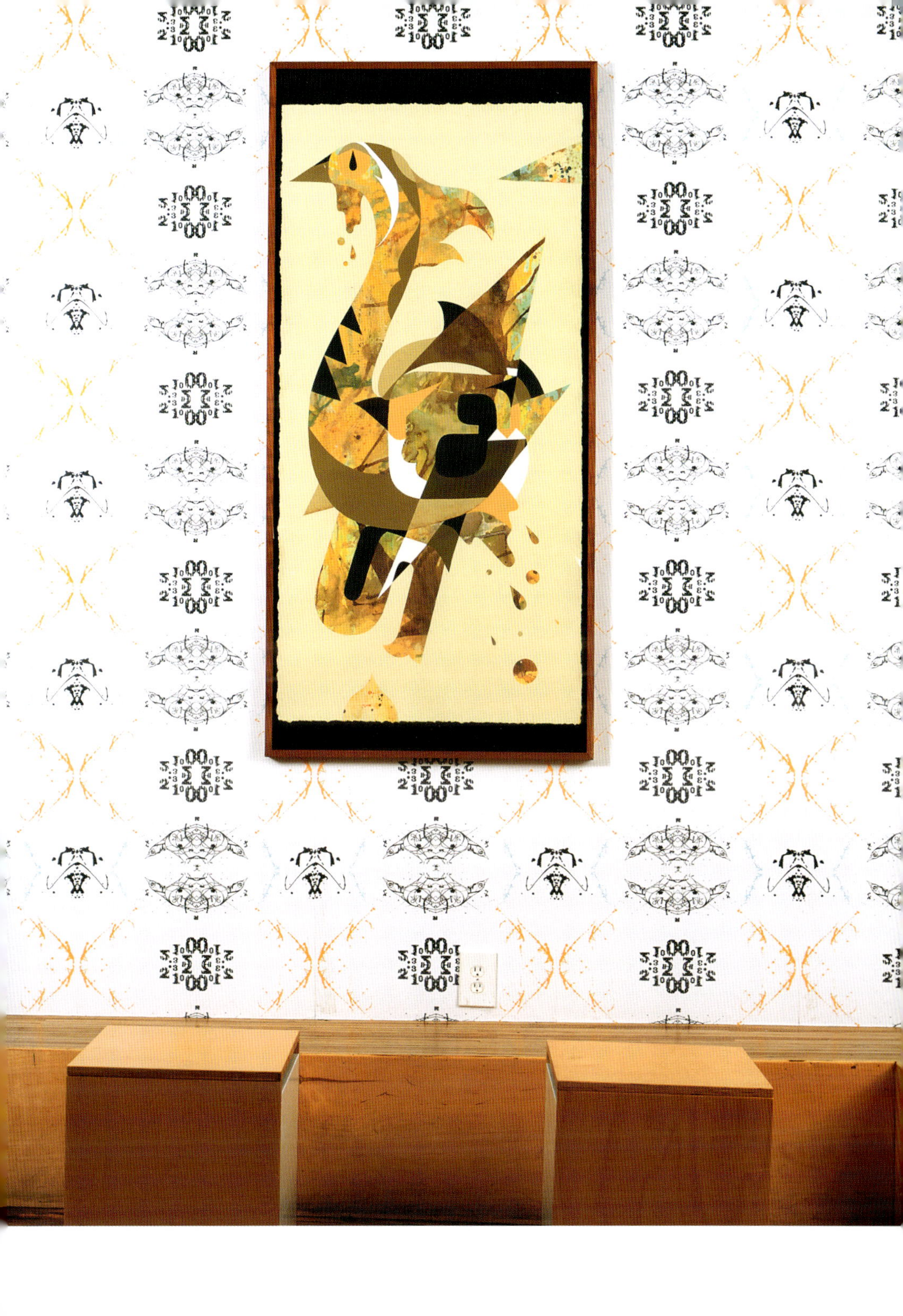

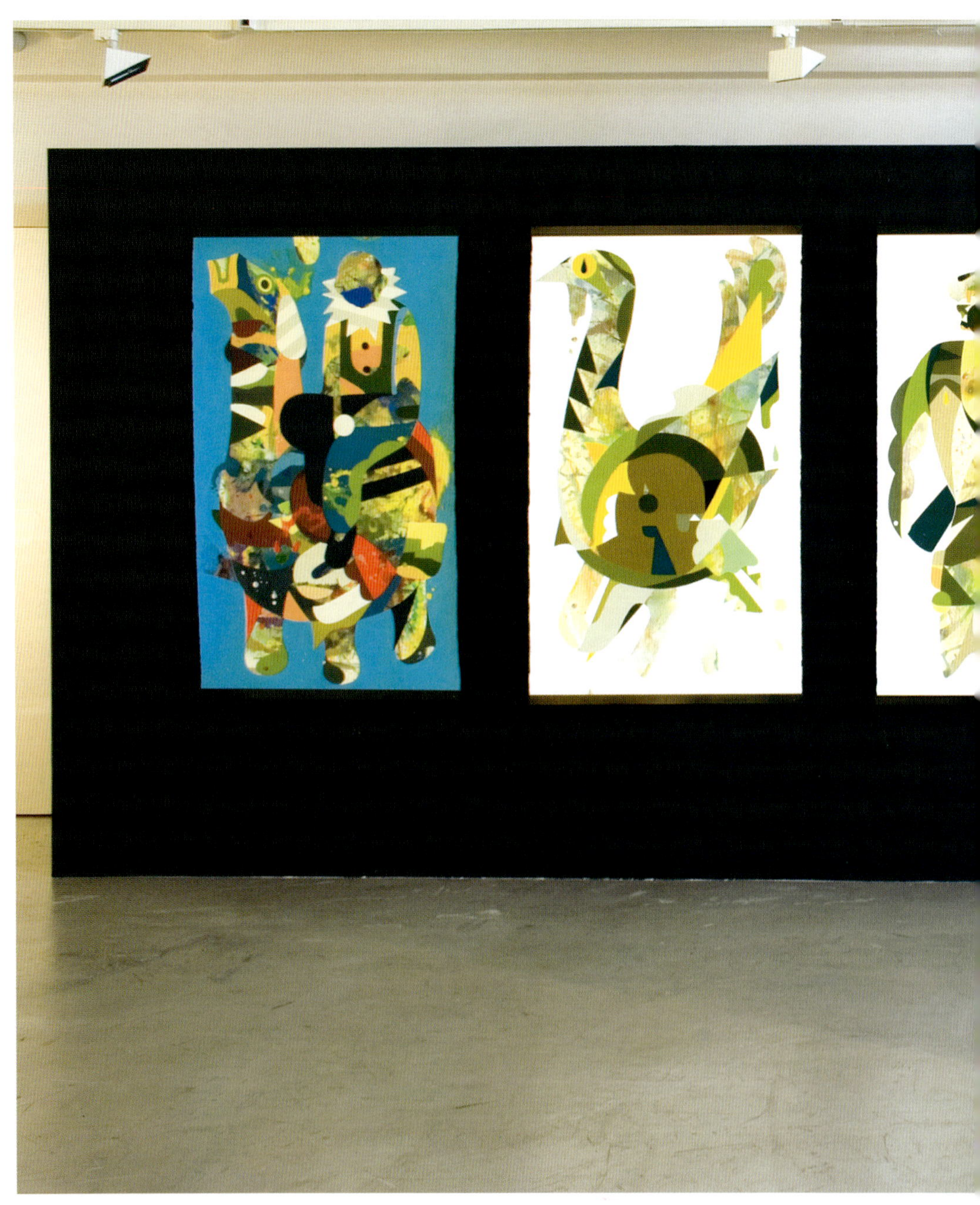

Hunter, 2006
Acrylic on paper, wood, metal, wire
87 x 236 x 23"

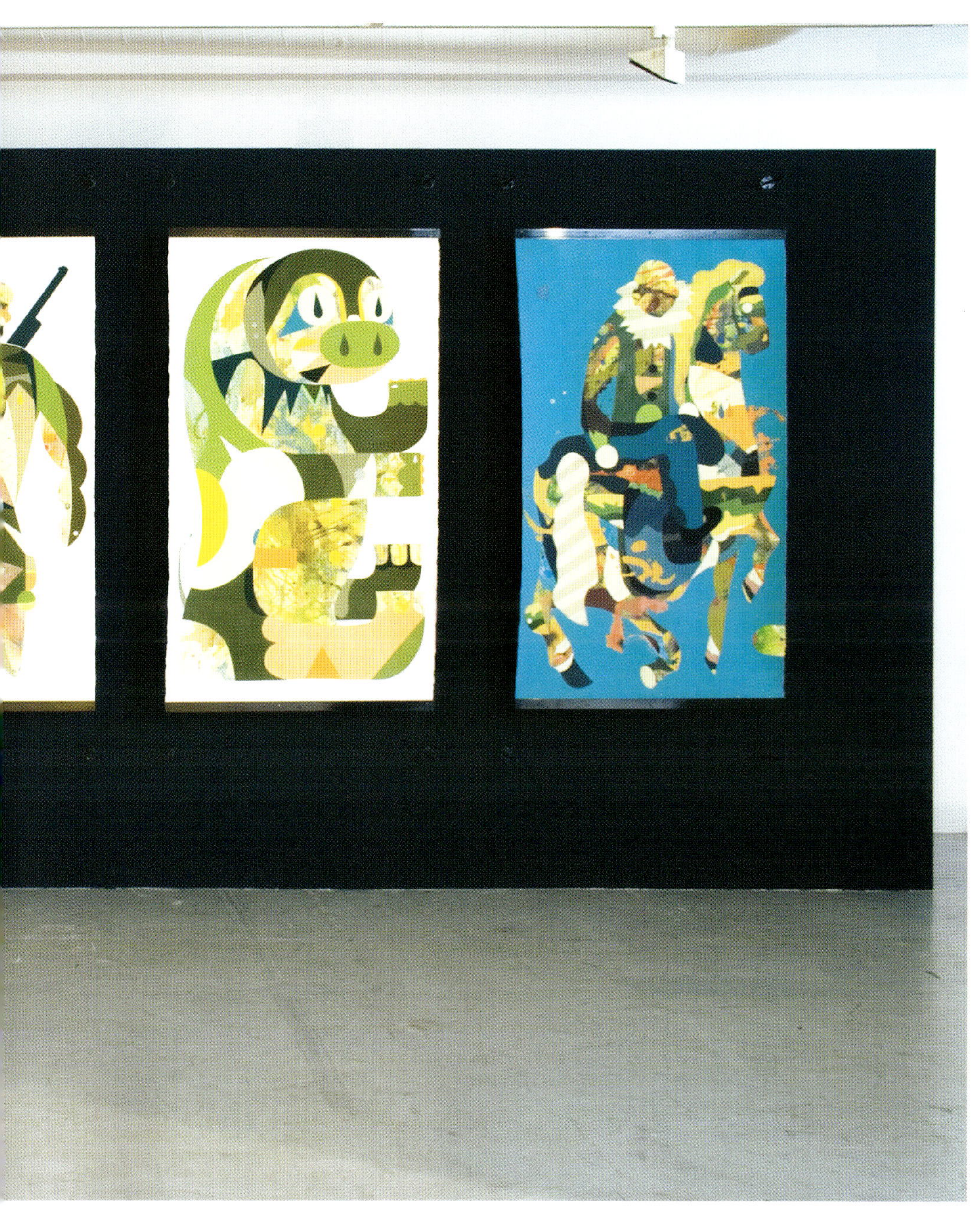

(detail of *Hunter*)

Hunter 1, 2006

Acrylic on paper

54 x 30"

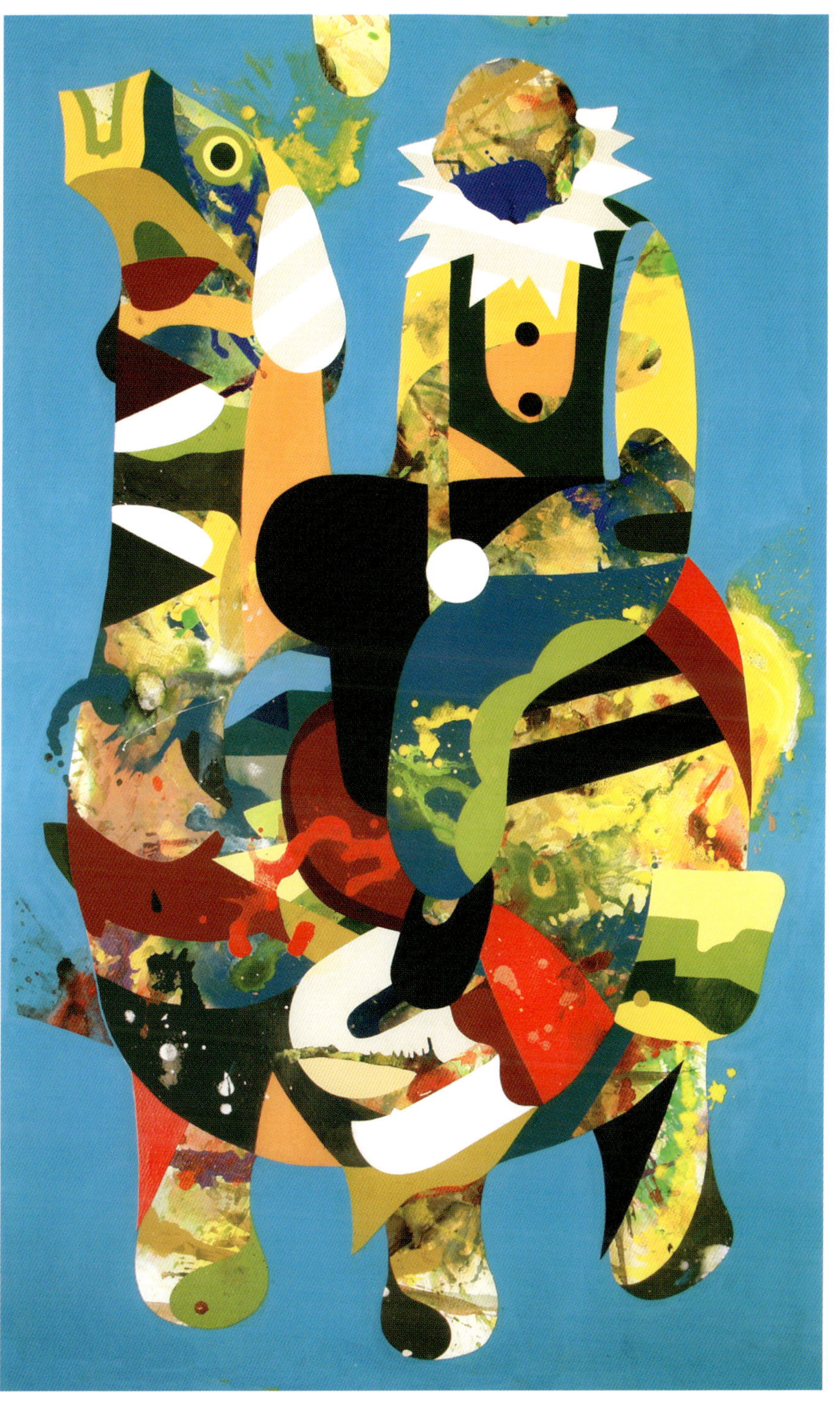

(detail of *Hunter*)
Being Hunted 1, 2006
Acrylic on paper
54 x 30"

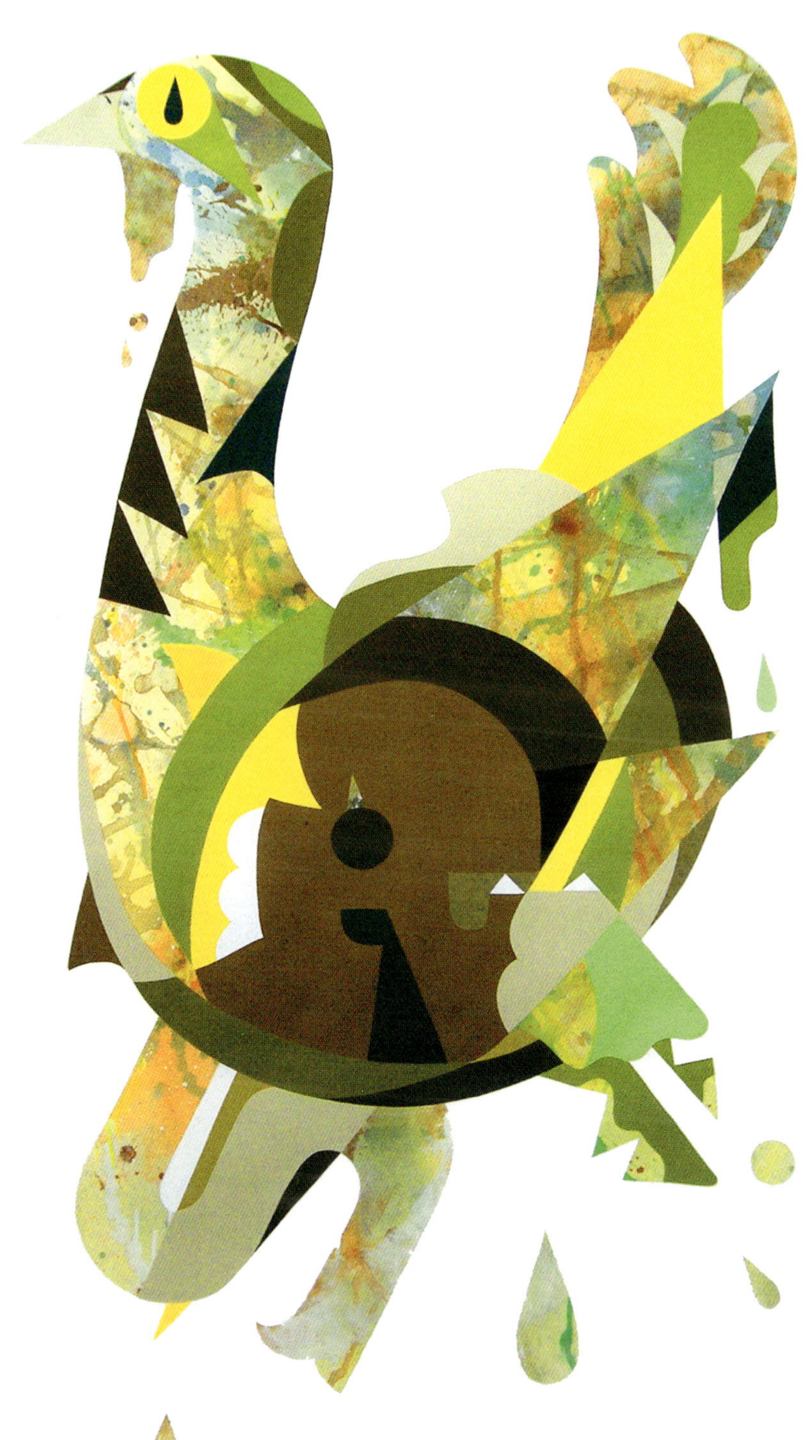

(detail of *Hunter*)
Hunter 2, 2006
Acrylic on paper
54 x 30"

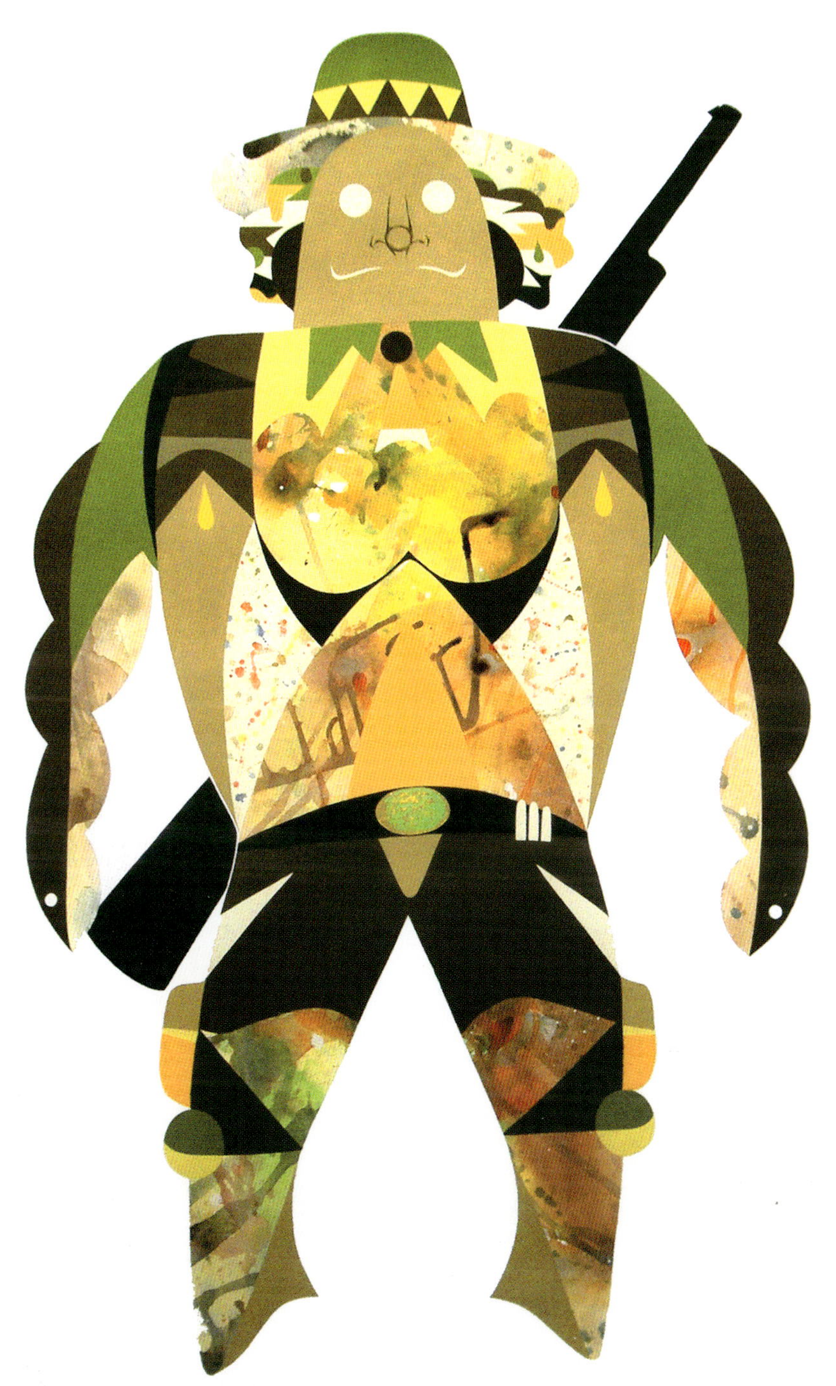

(detail of *Hunter*)
Being Hunted 2, 2006
Acrylic on paper
54 x 30"

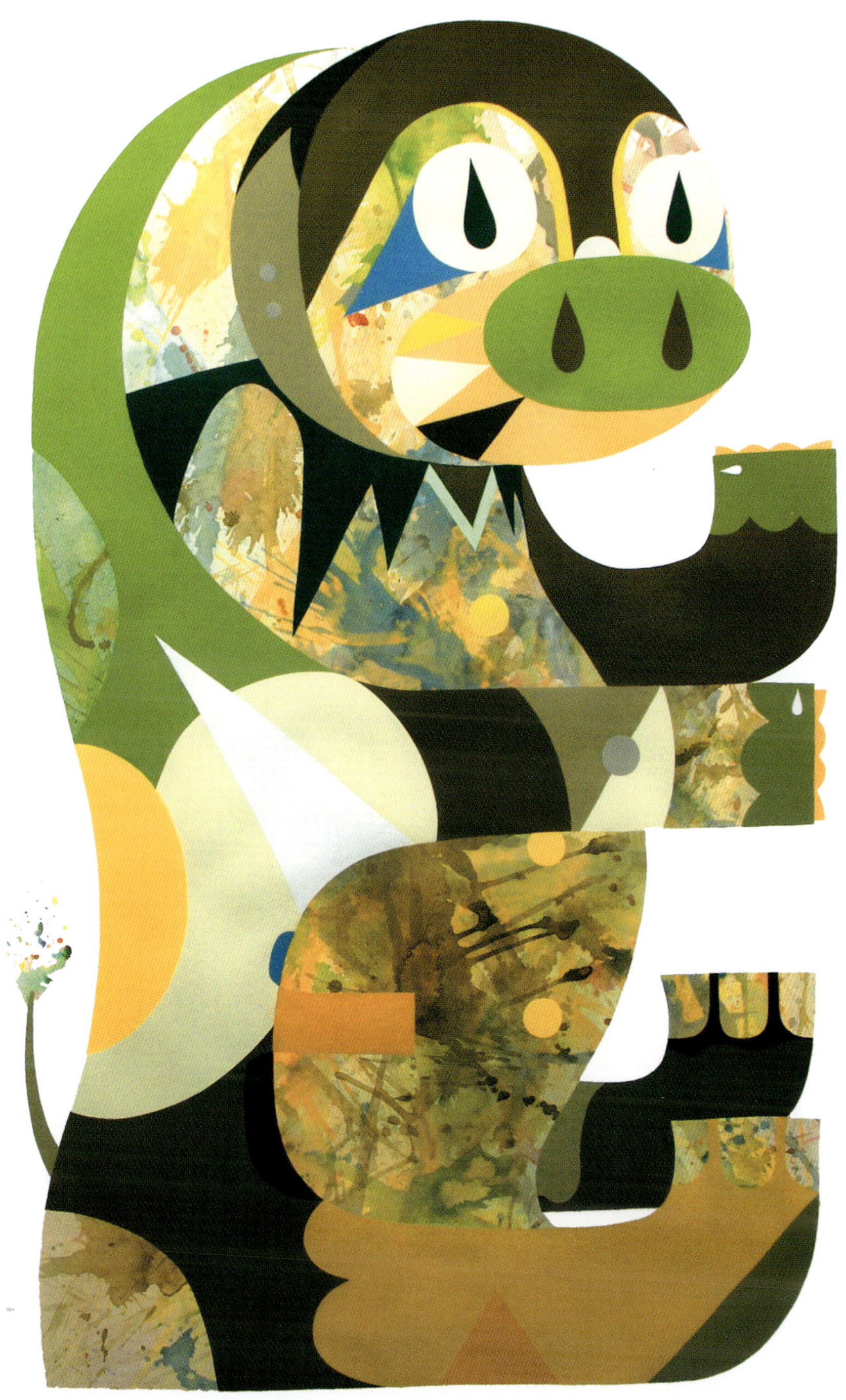

(detail of *Hunter*)

Hunter 3, 2006

Acrylic on paper

54 x 30"

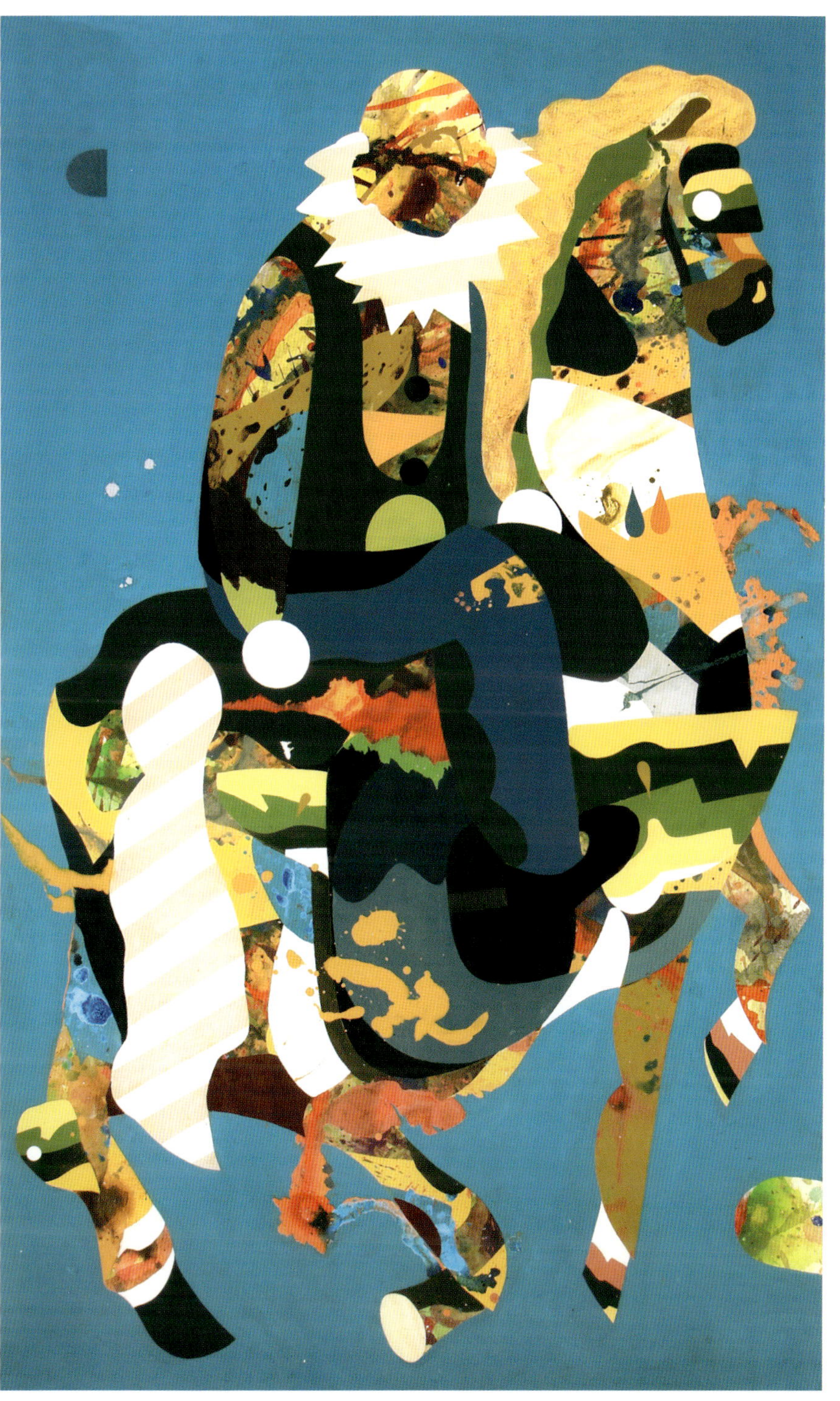

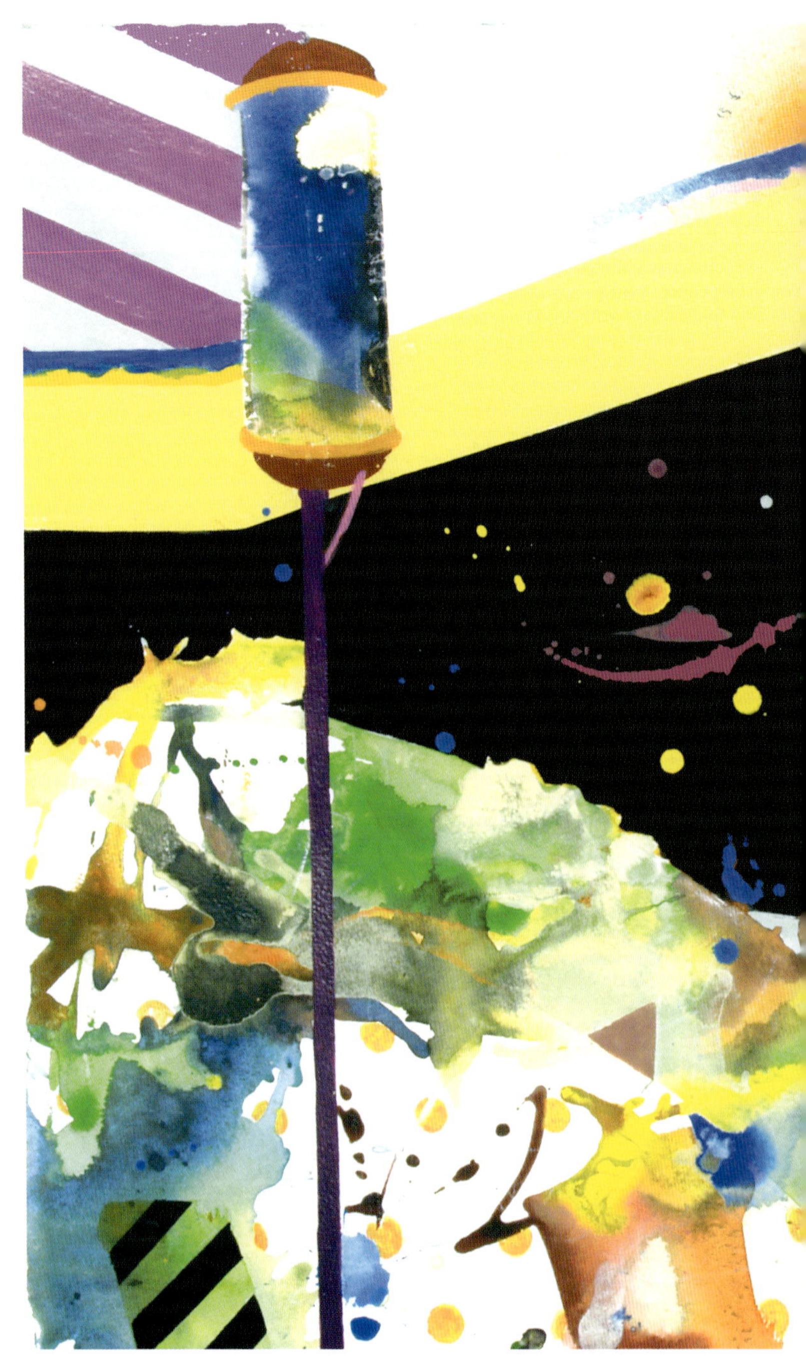

Under the Light, 2006
Acrylic on paper
20 x 29"

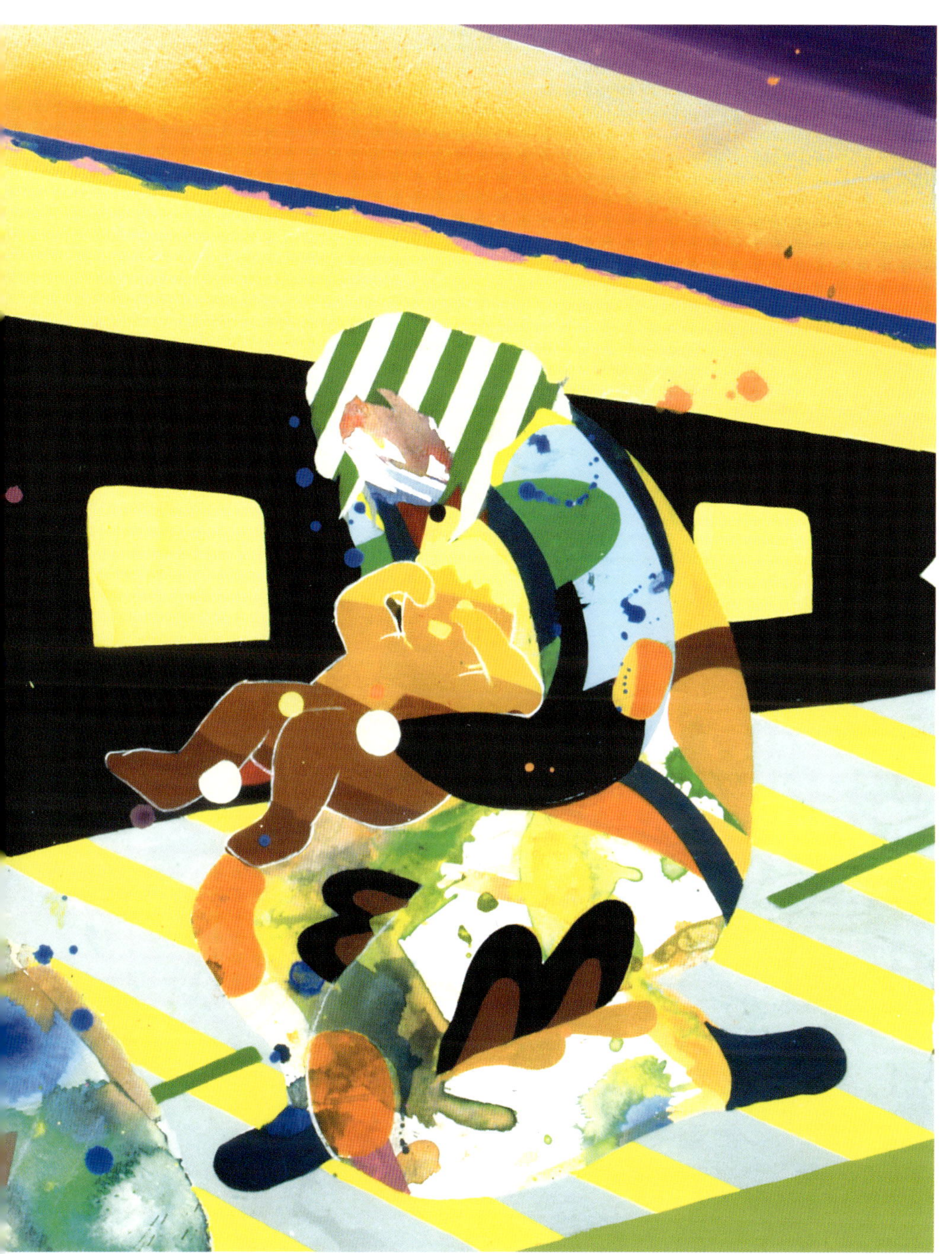

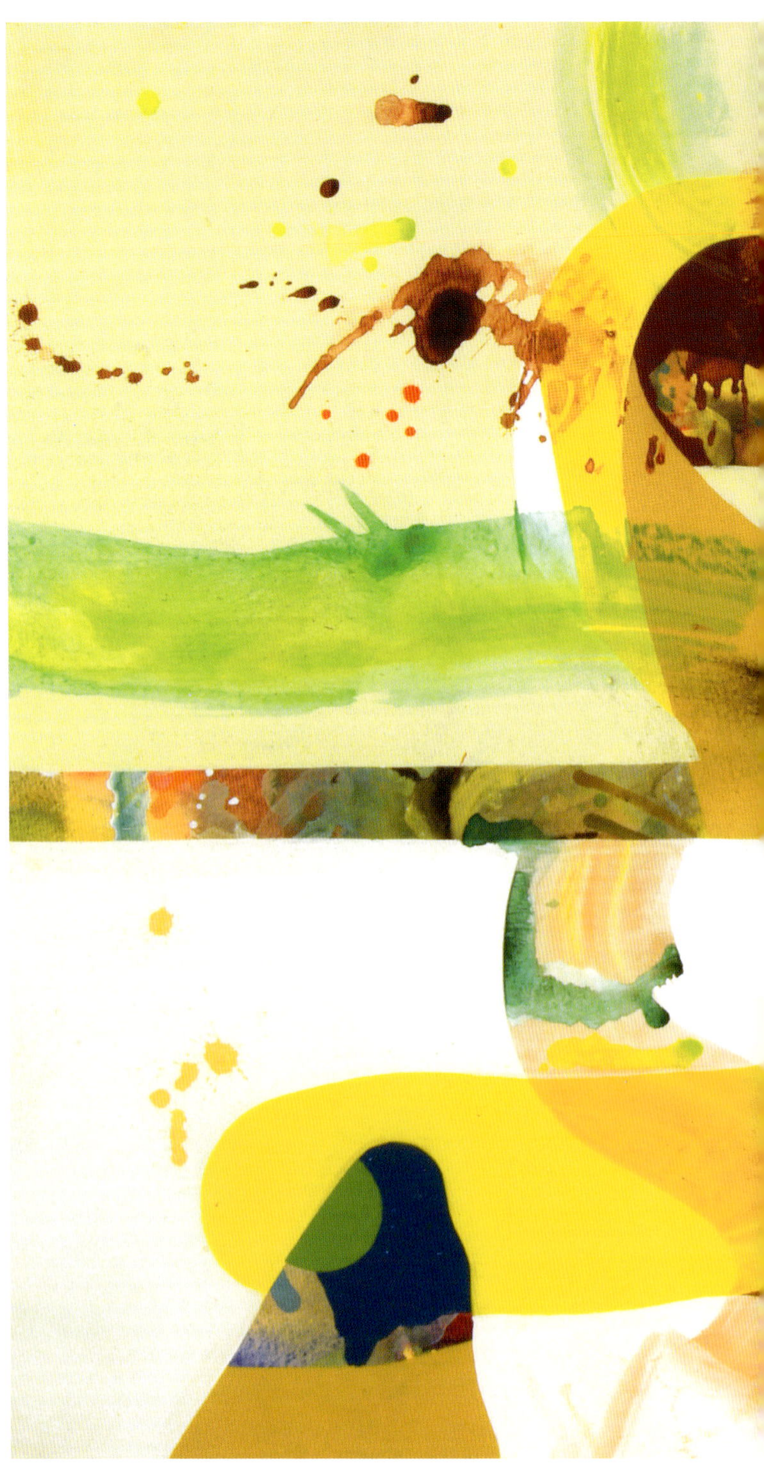

Fluidity, 2006
Acrylic on paper
30 x 40"

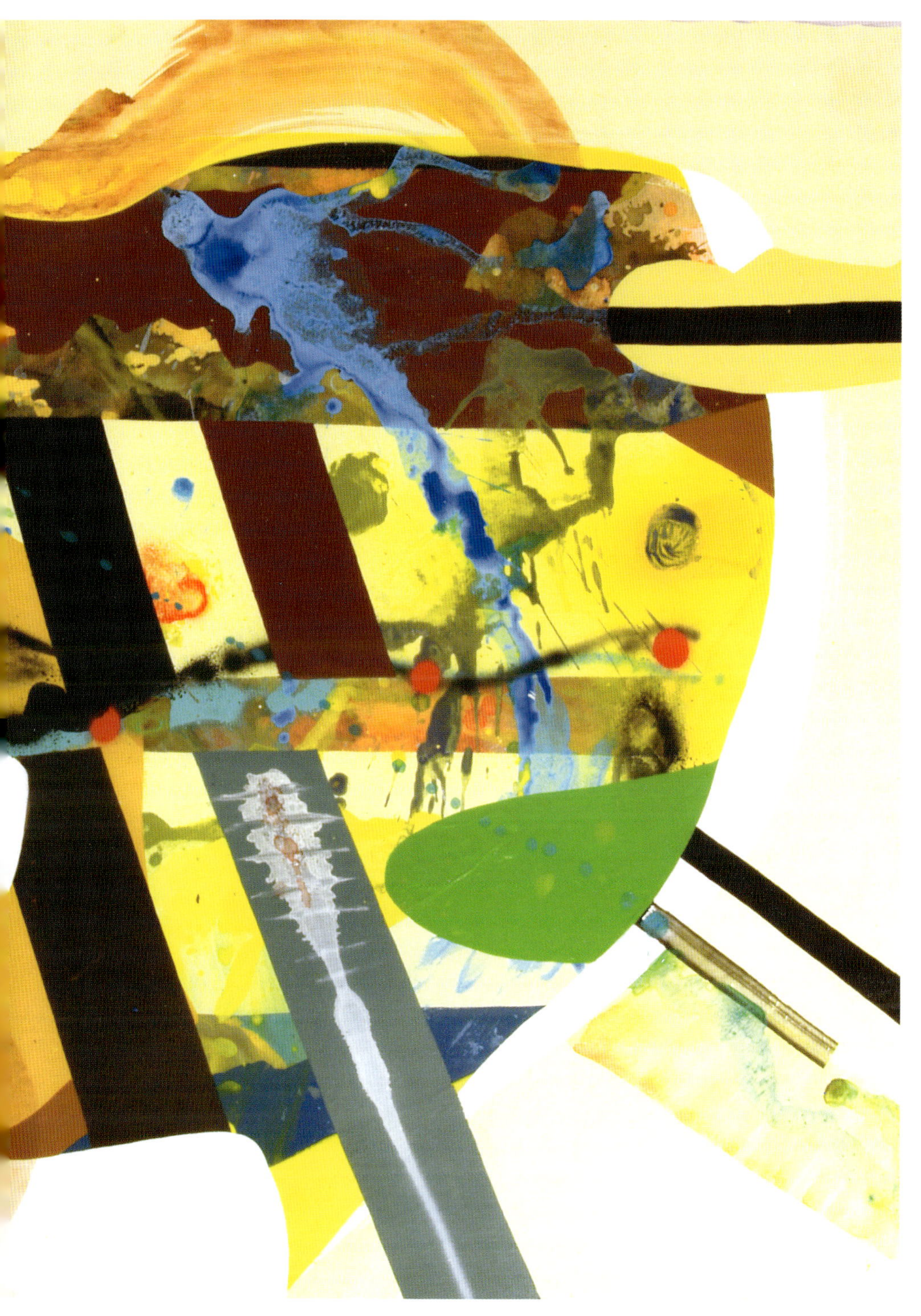

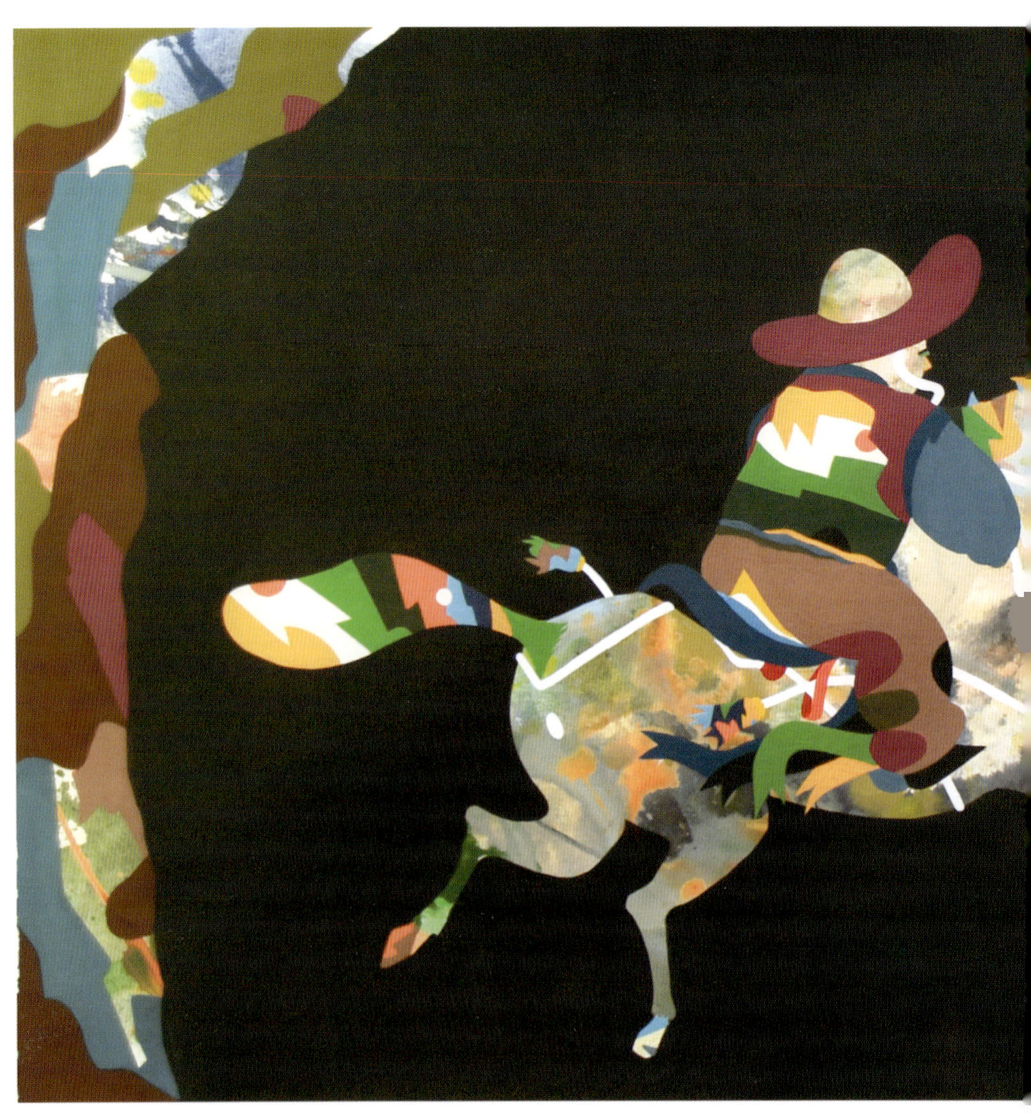

Collabotal, 2006
Acrylic on paper
18 x 35"

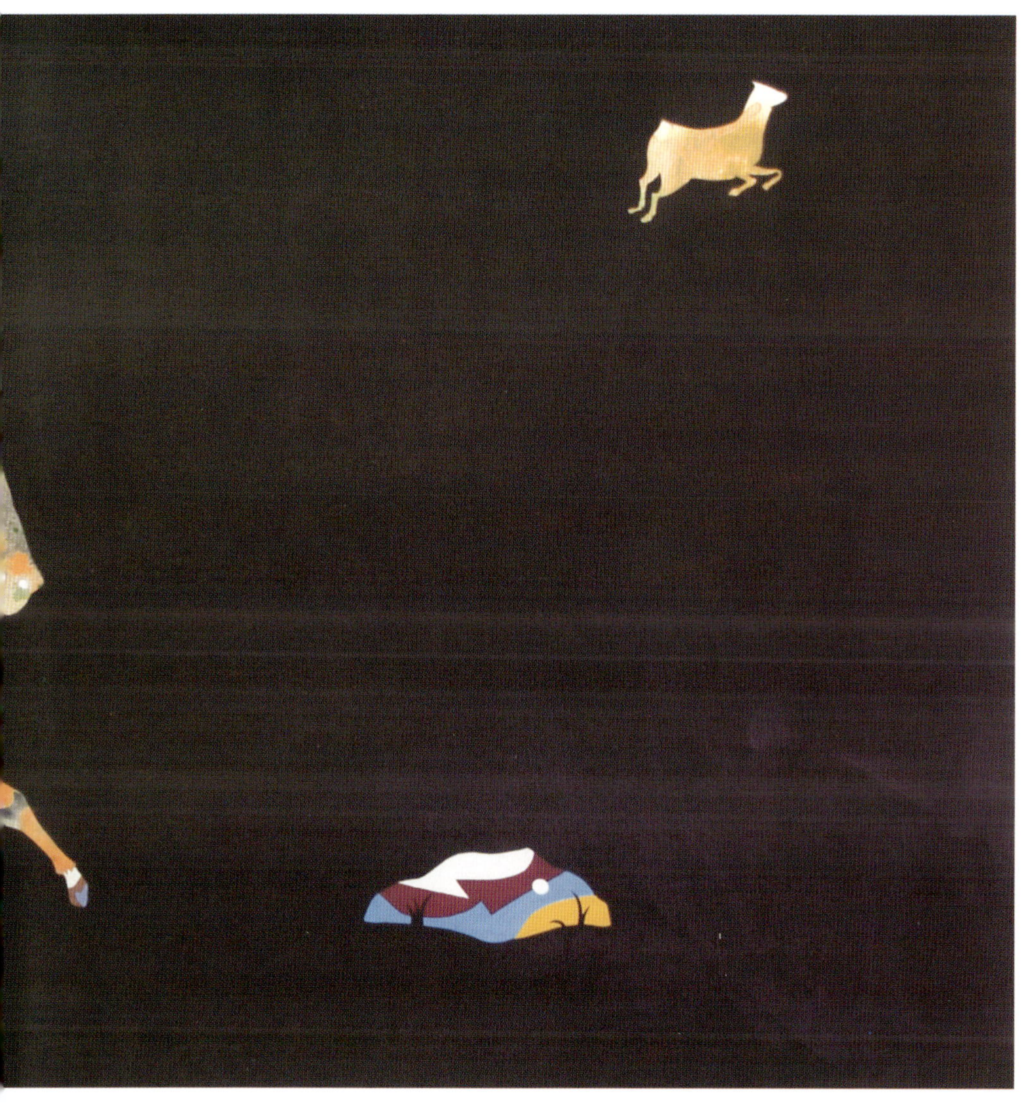

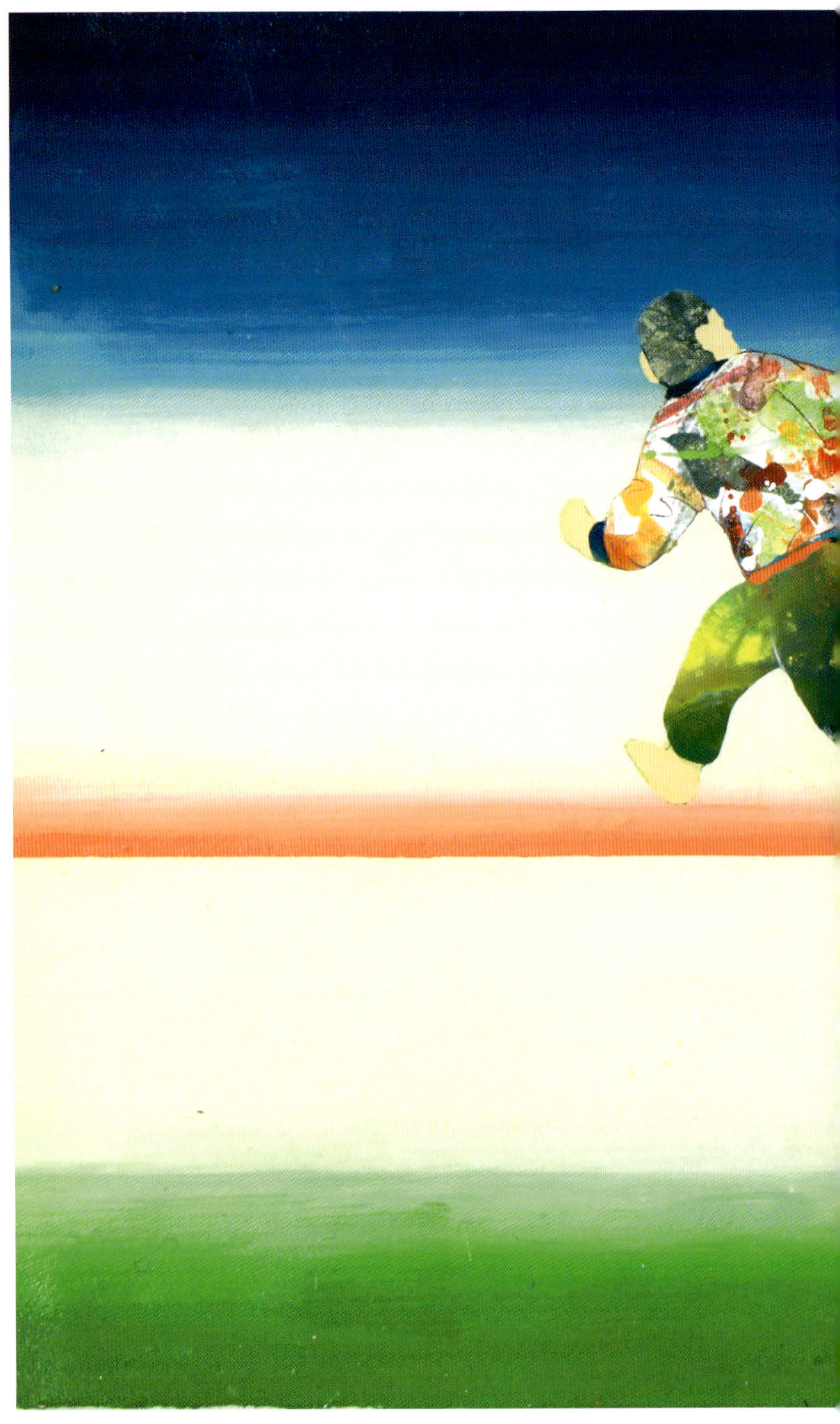

Runnin', 2006
Acrylic on paper
20 x 29"

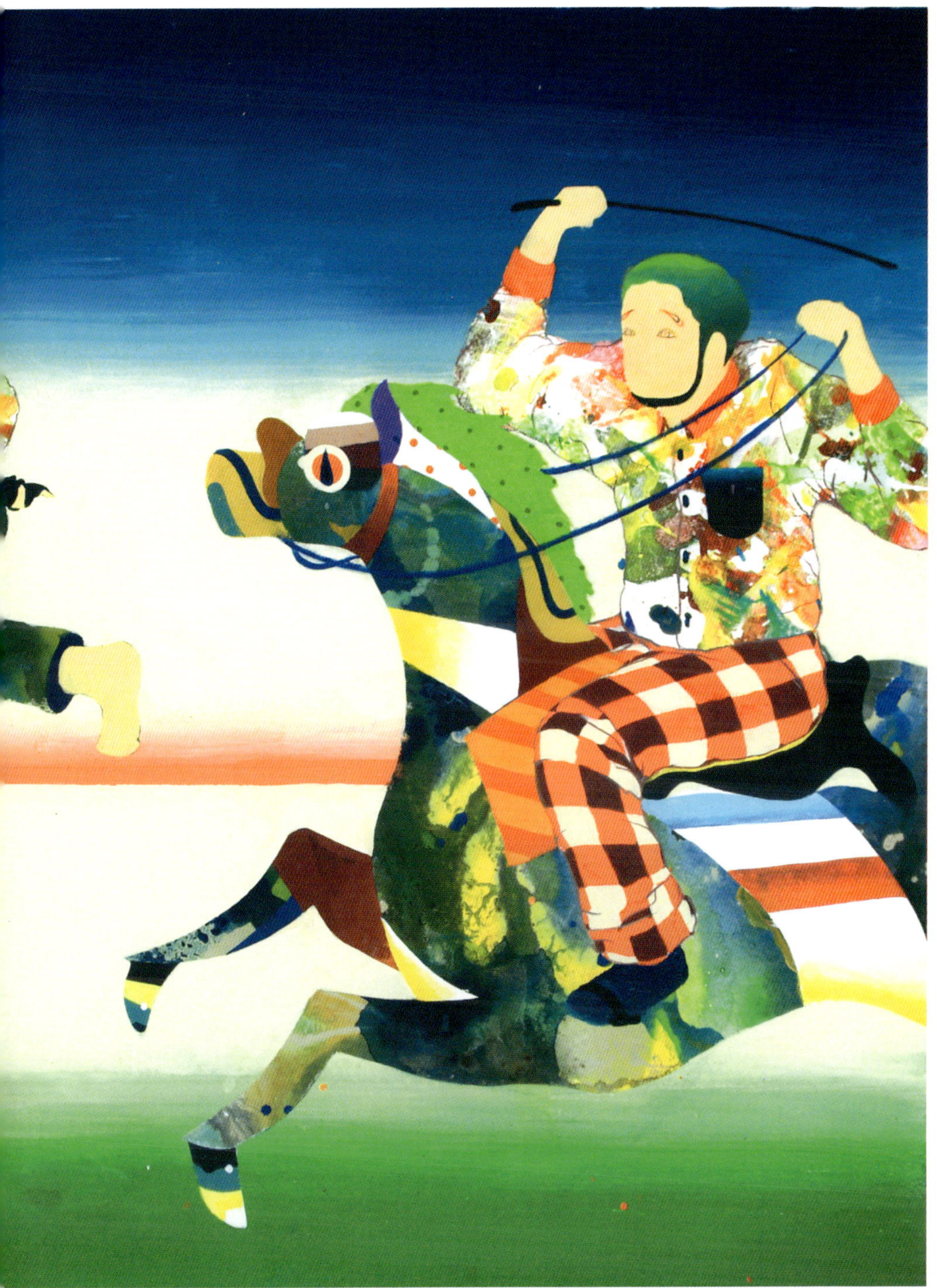

Partia, 2005
Acrylic on paper
18 x 24"

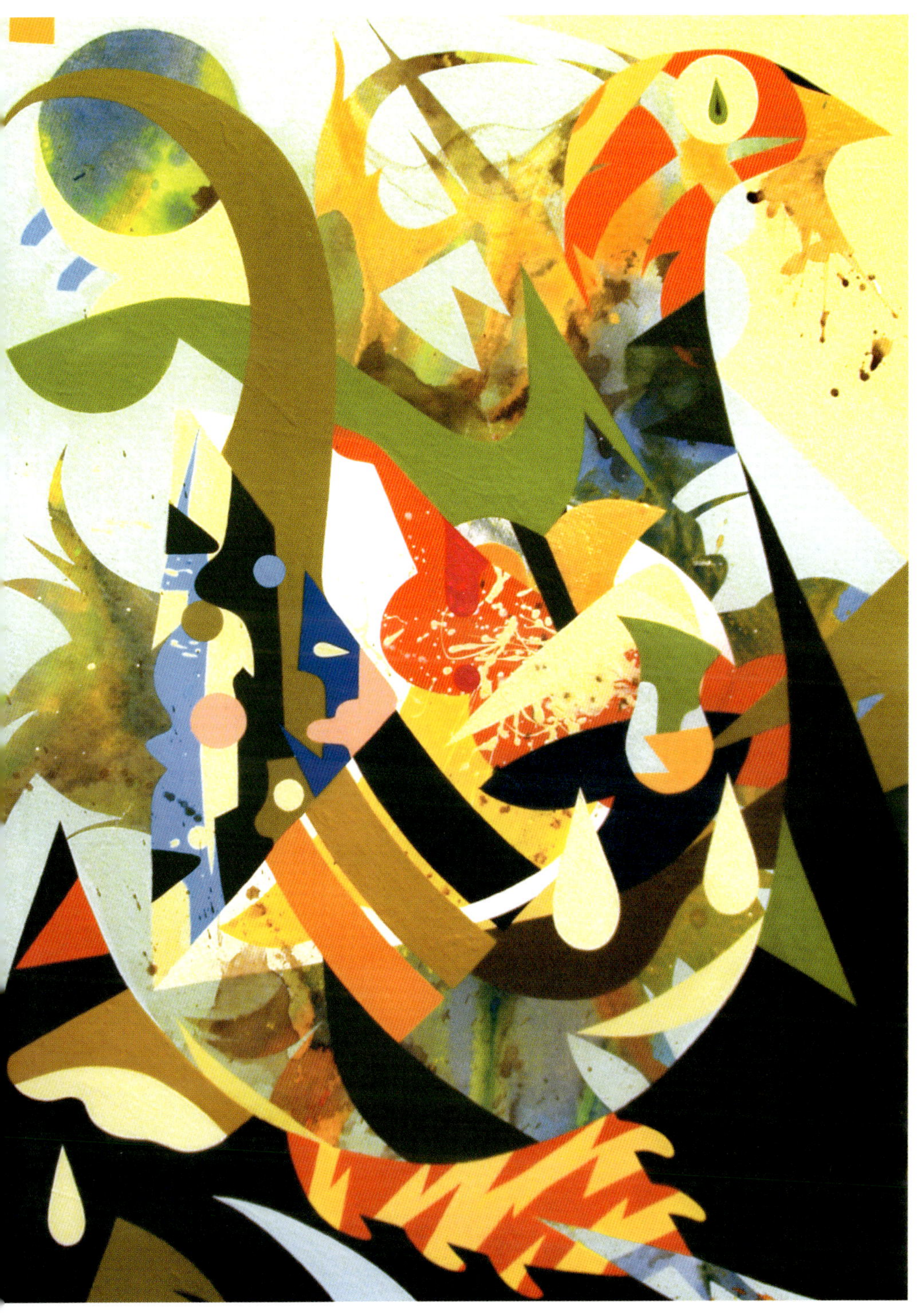

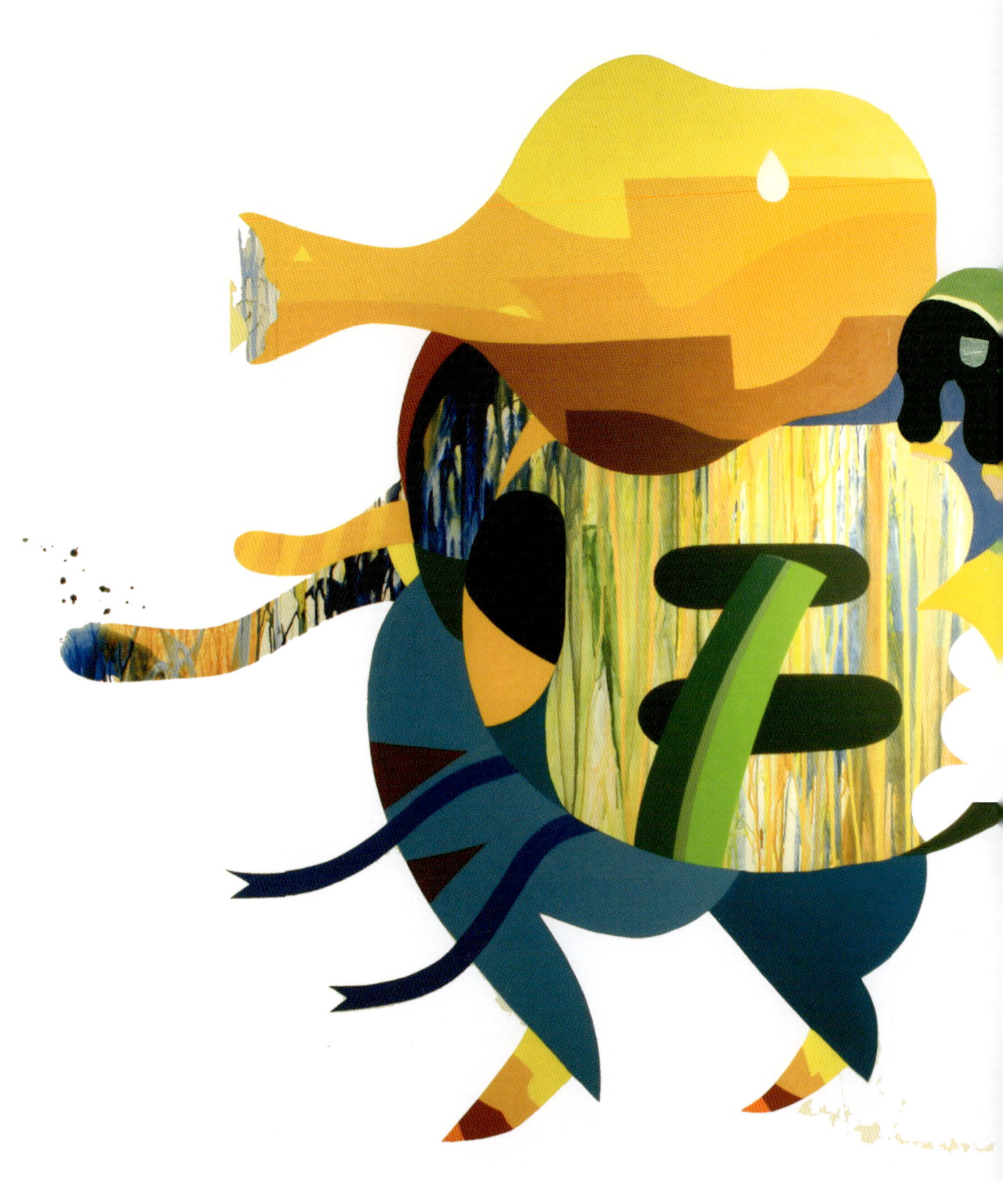

Details of *Three Ochre*, 2005
Acrylic on wood panel
87 x 275 x 2.5"

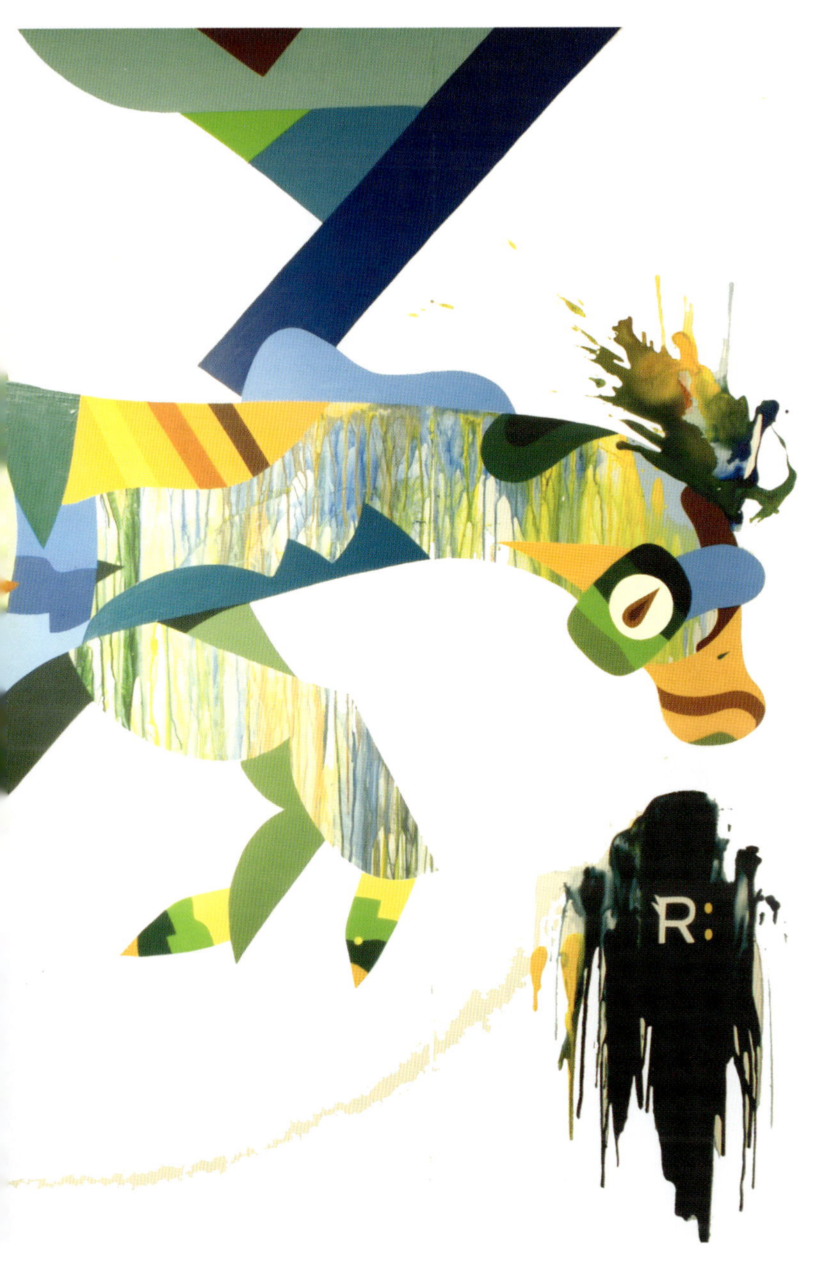
R:

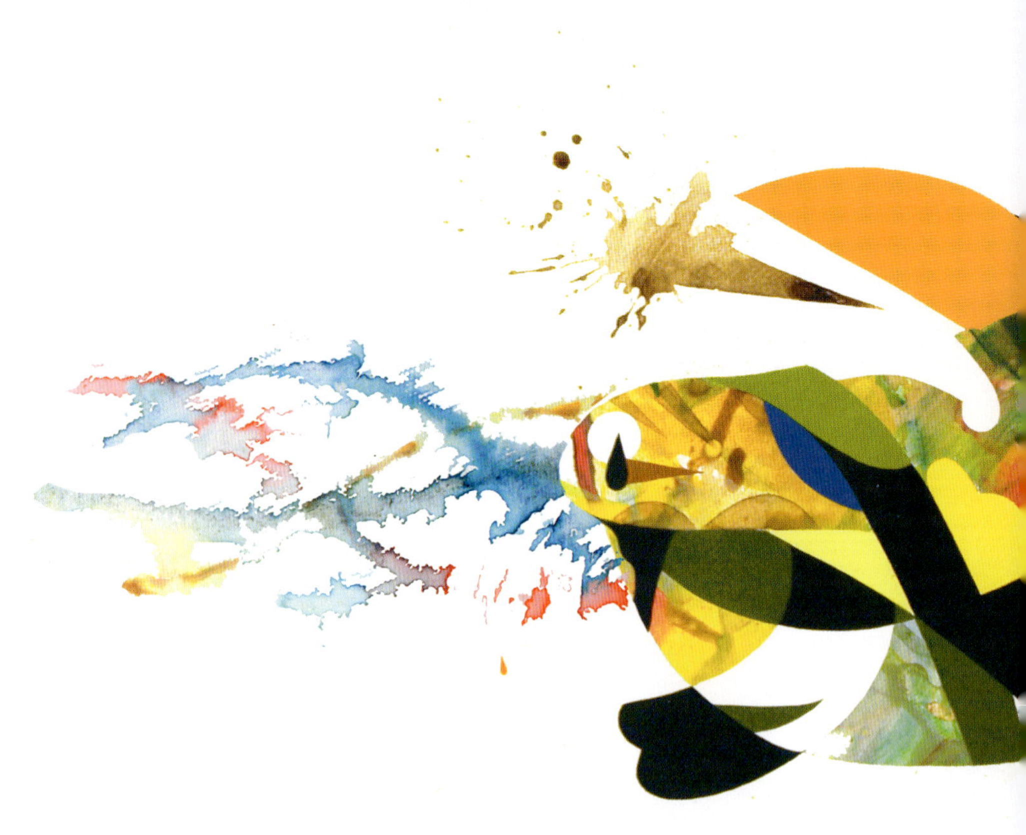

Mouting, 2006
Acrylic on paper
12 x 27"

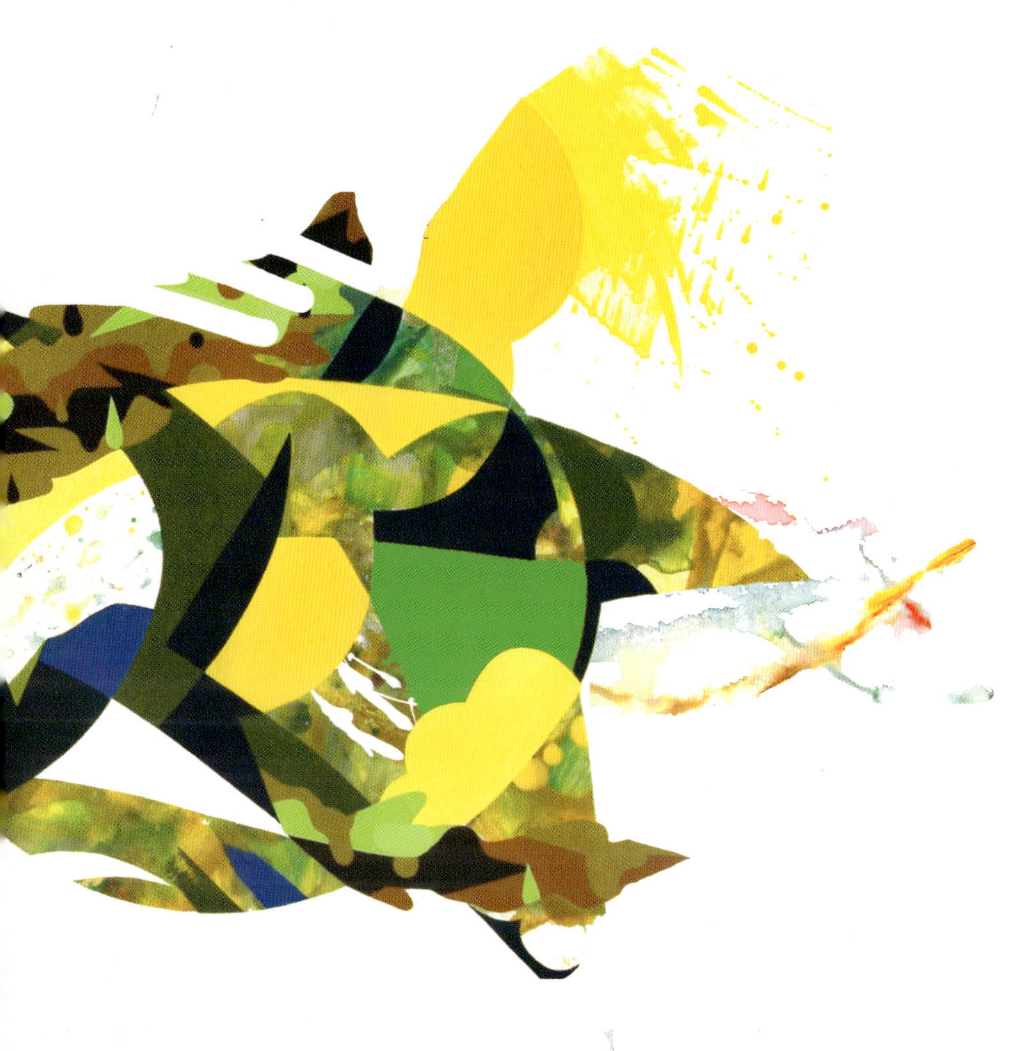

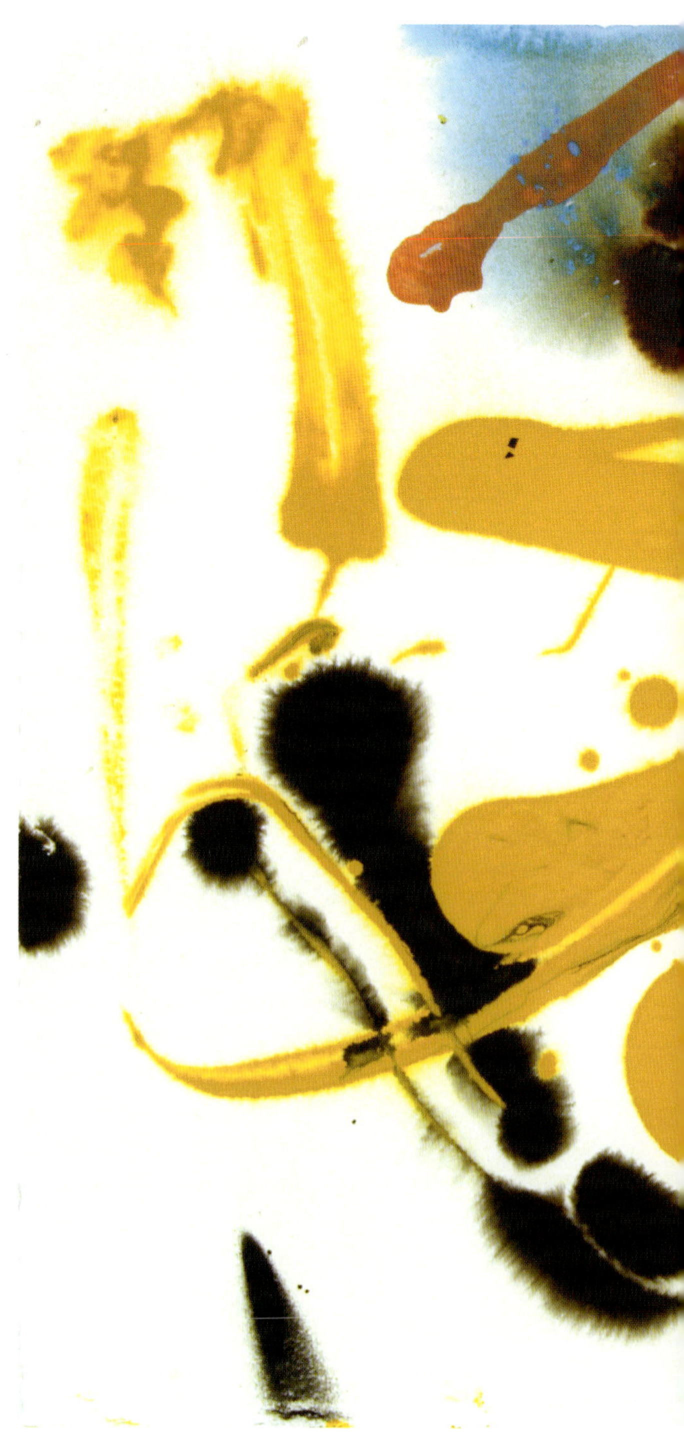

Still Sequence, 2006
Acrylic on paper
15 x 20"

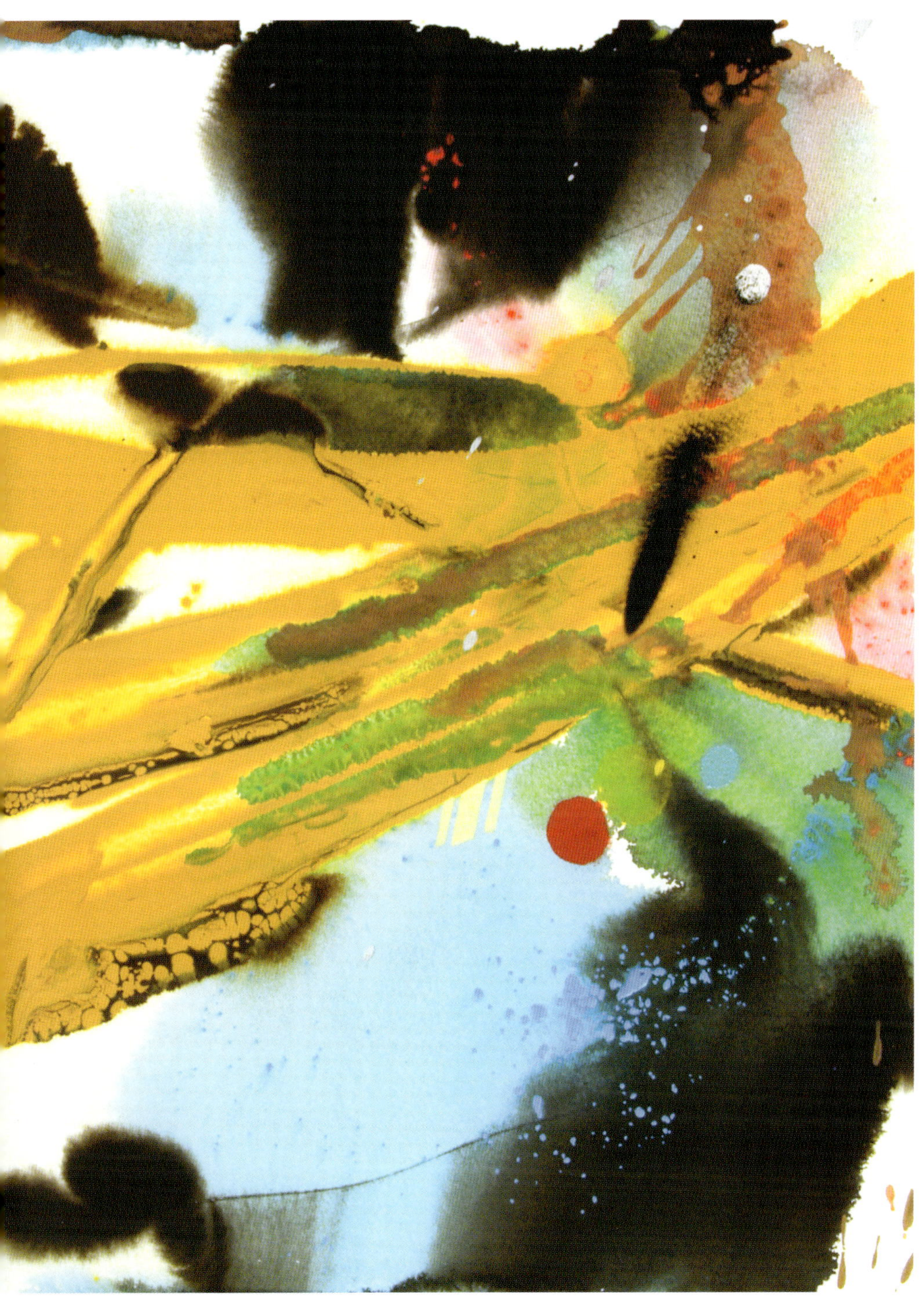

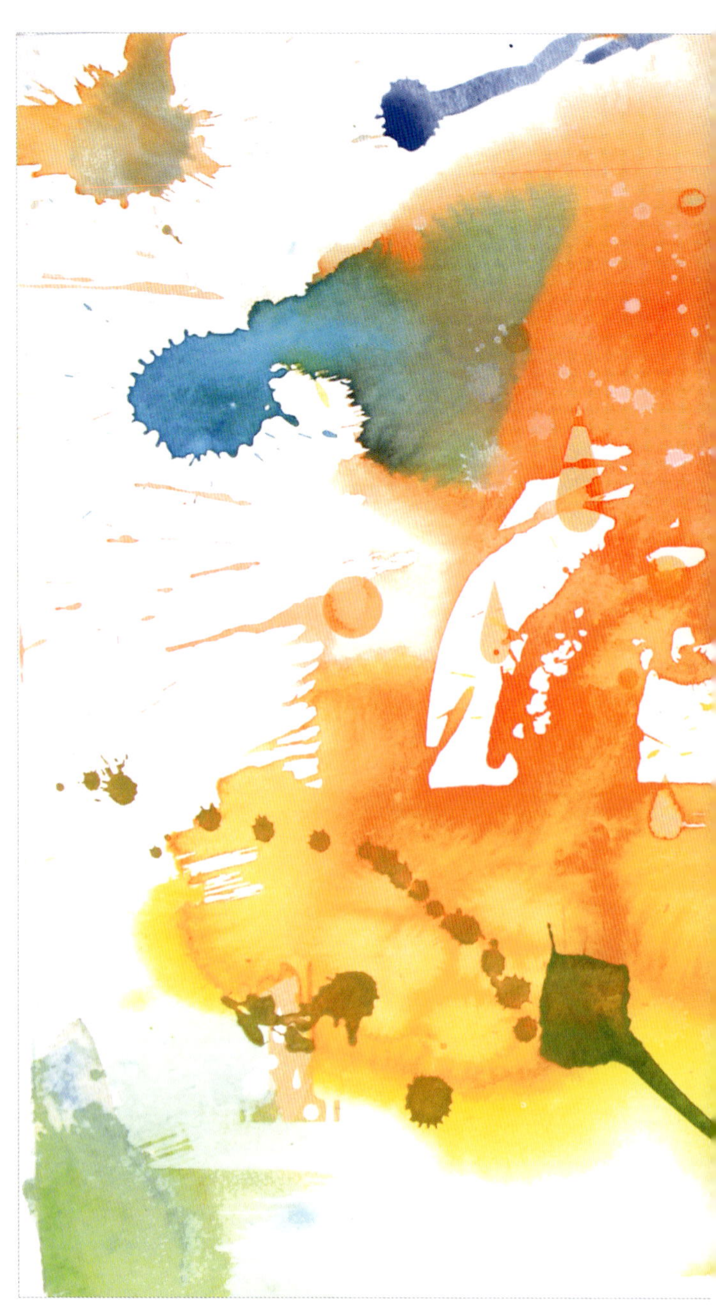

Re-incarnation, 2005
Water color and acrylic on paper
28 x 43"

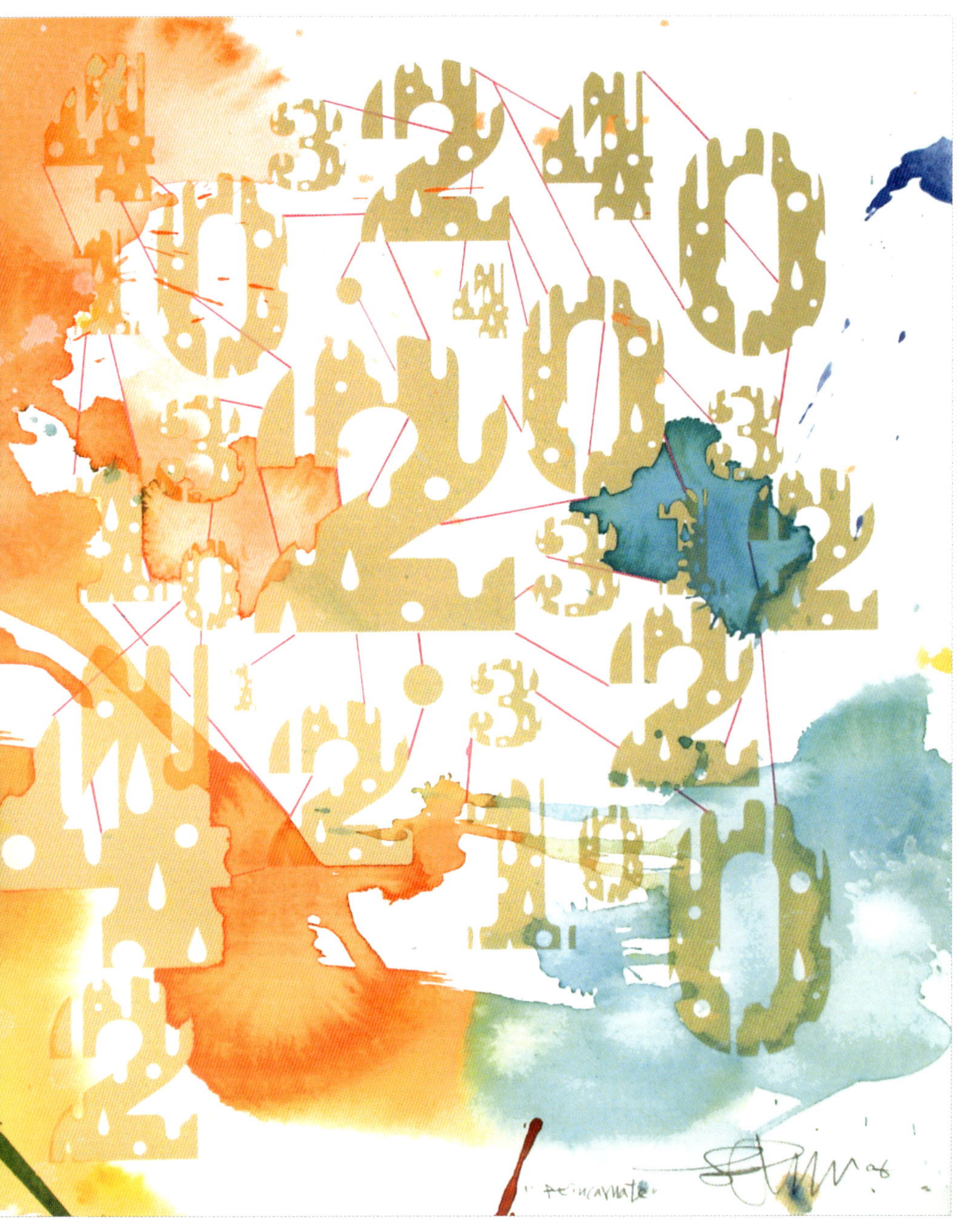
"reincarnate"

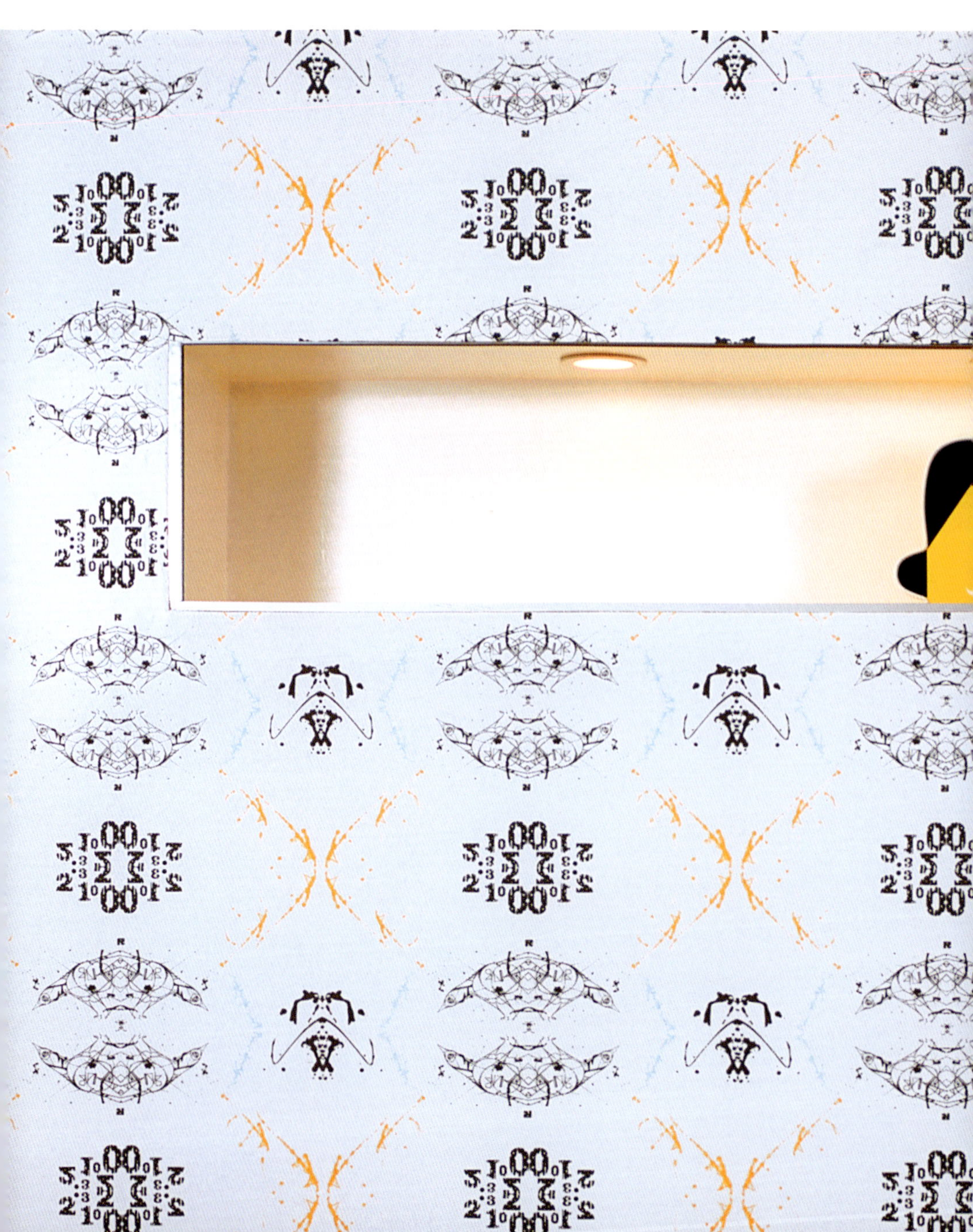

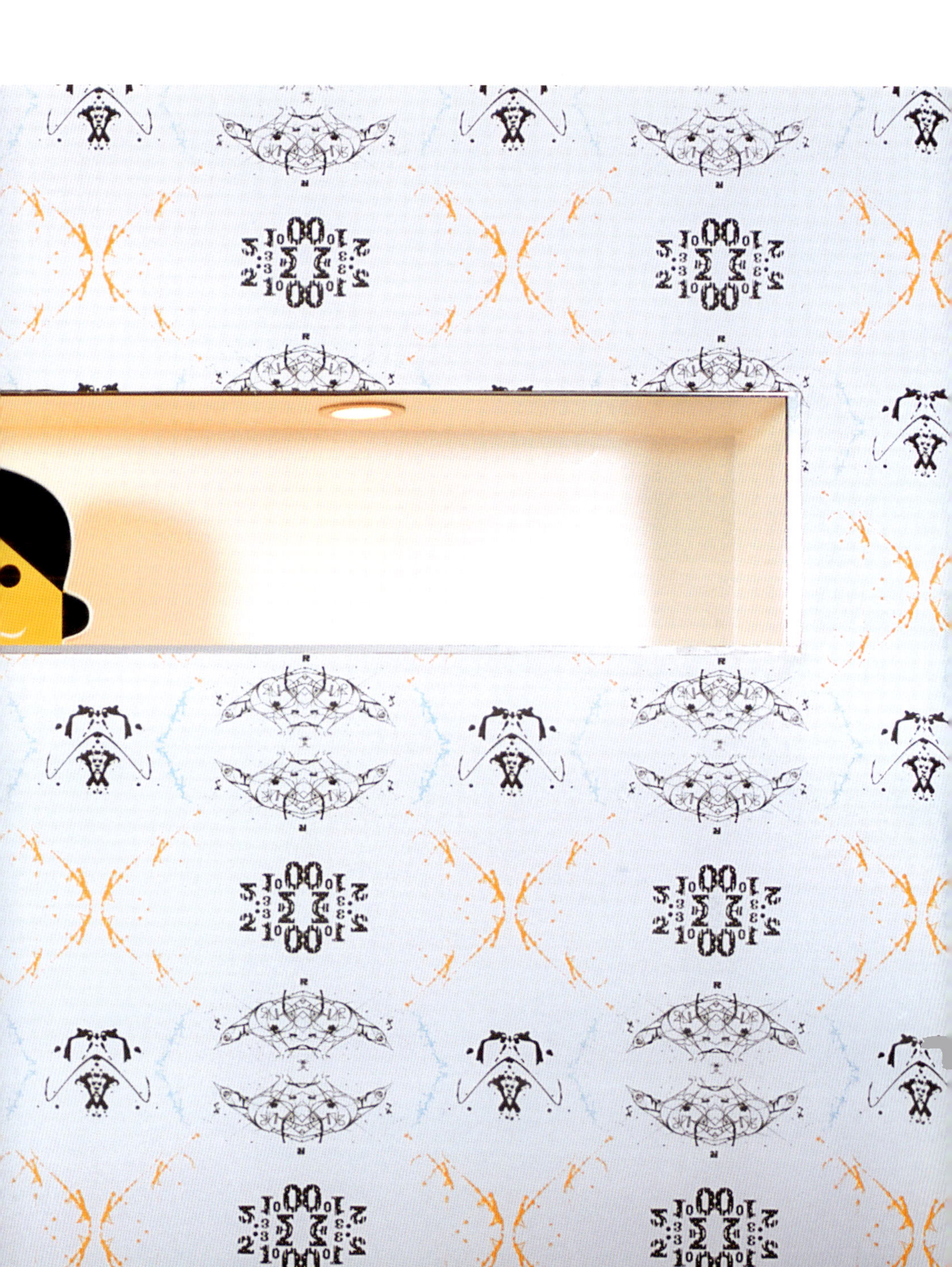

(previous page)
RLC in the Box, 2005
Plastic, metal, wood, silk screen wallpaper, light bulb
84 x 108"

(right page)
Unity, 2005
Latex on Concrete
Bedford Avenue, Brooklyn, NY

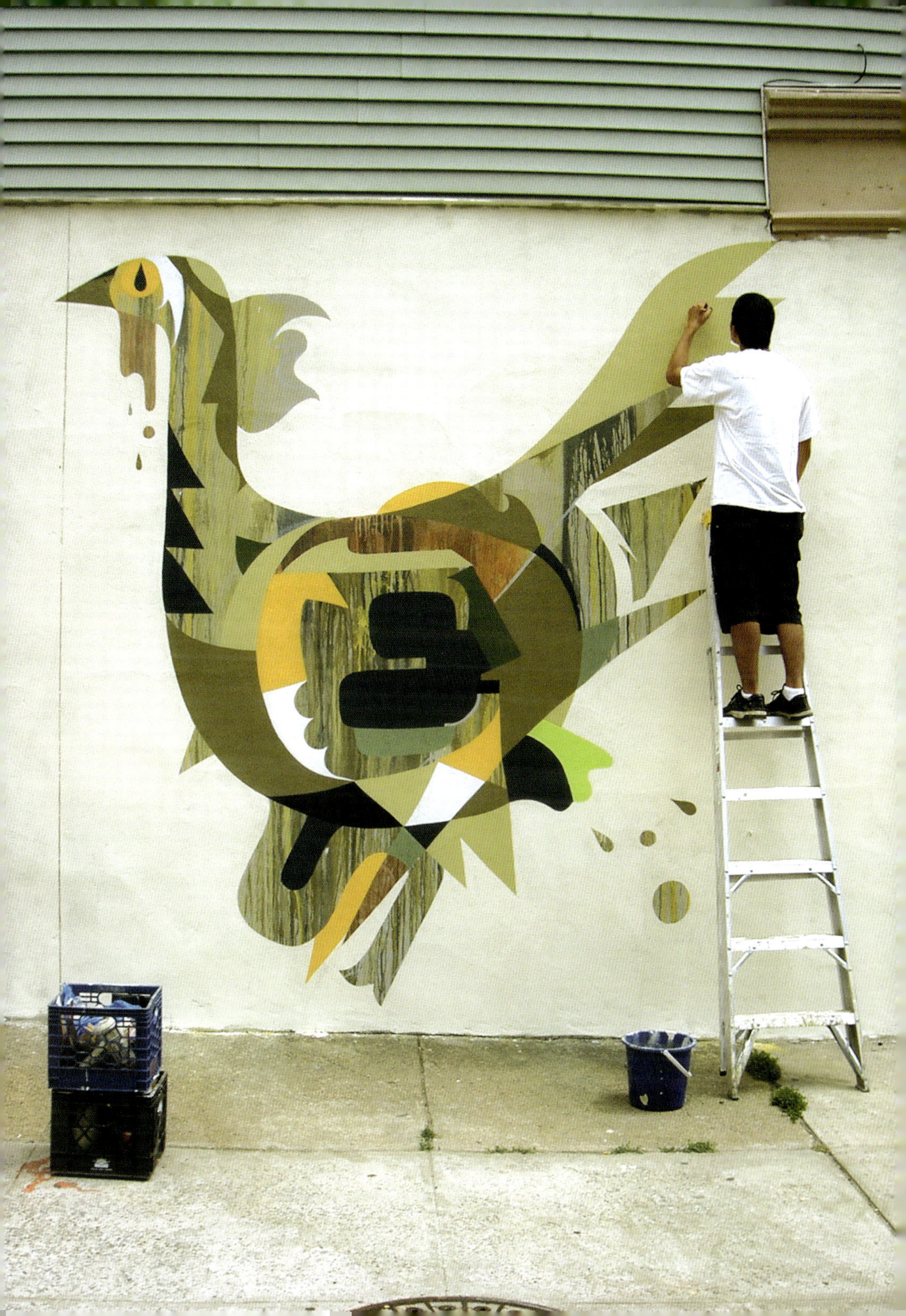

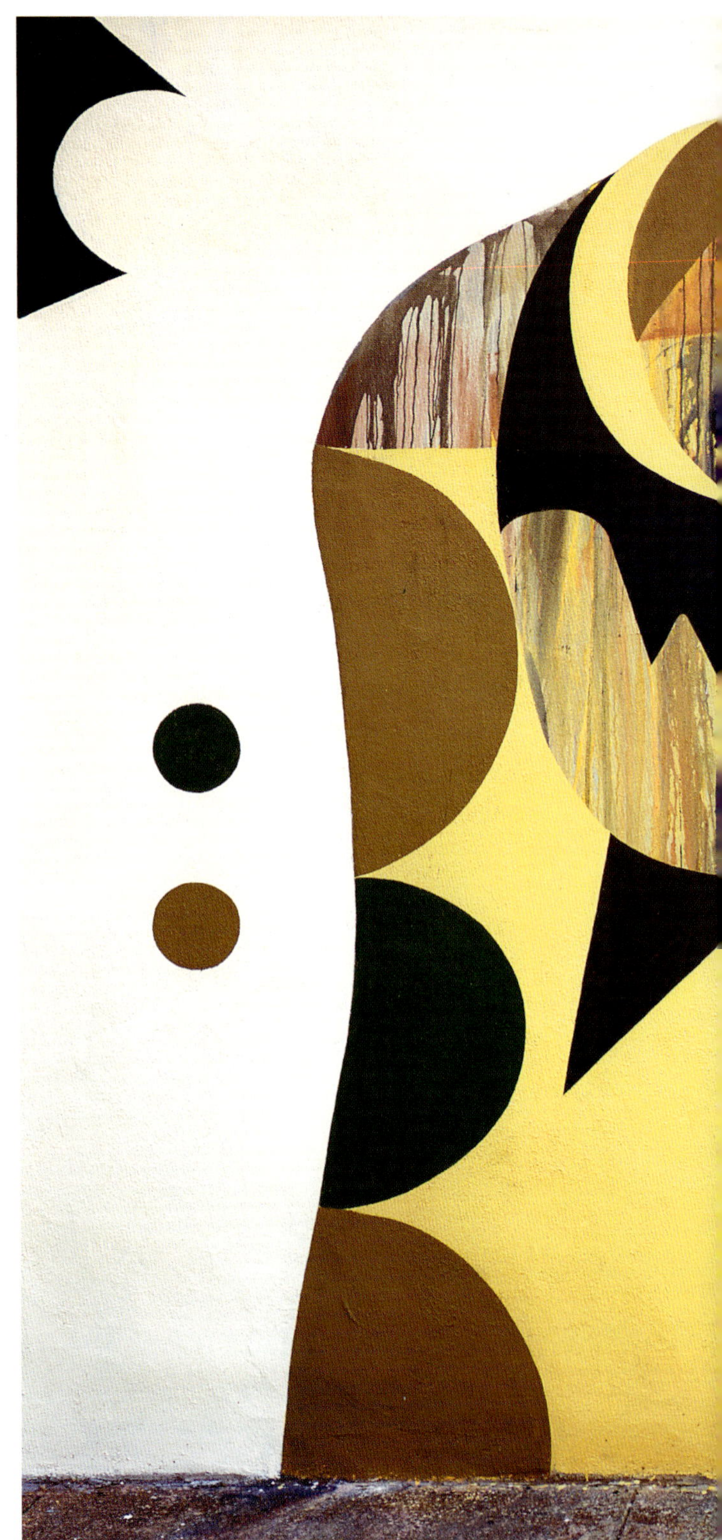

Unity, 2005
Latex on Concrete,
Bedford Avenue, Brooklyn, NY

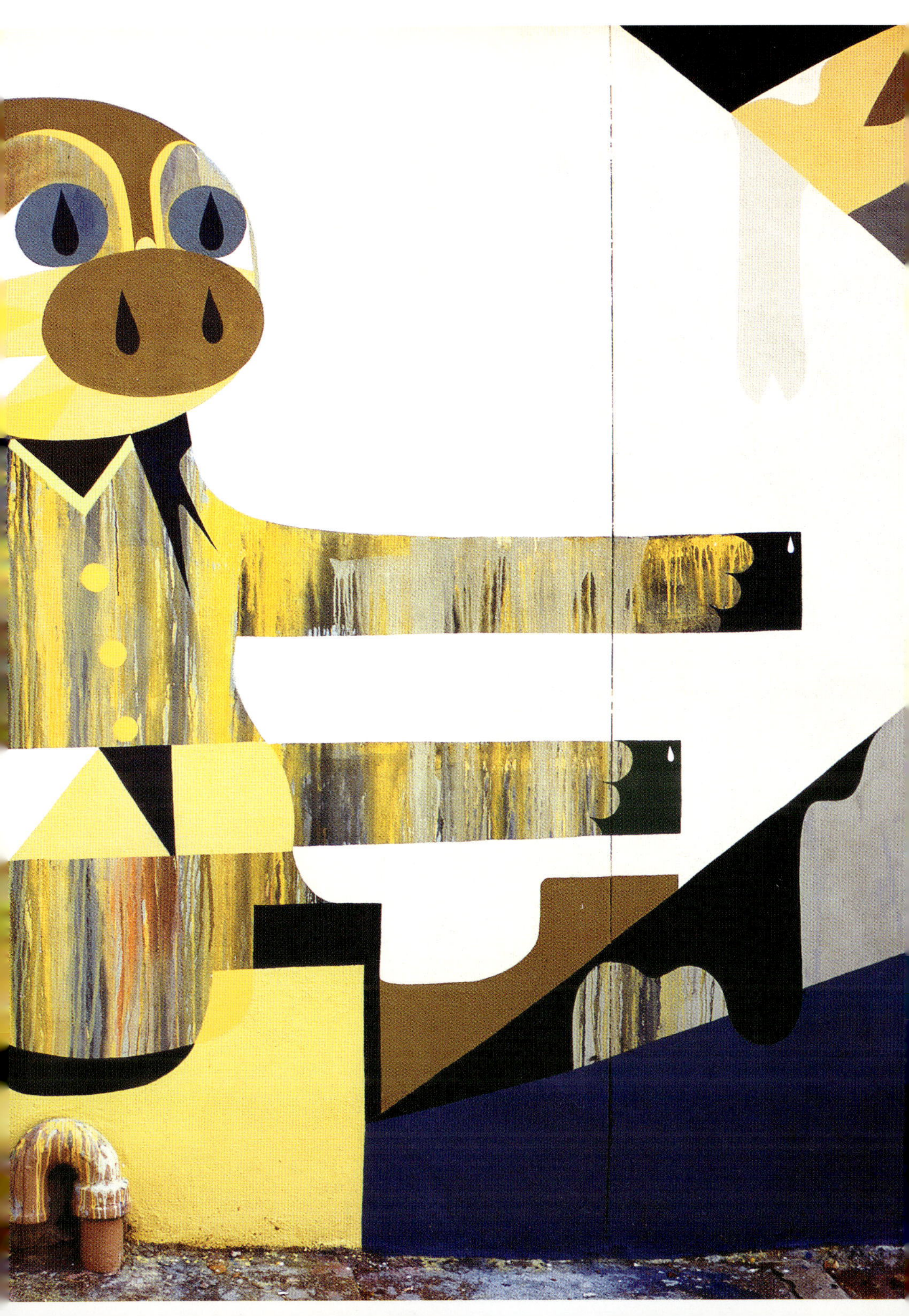

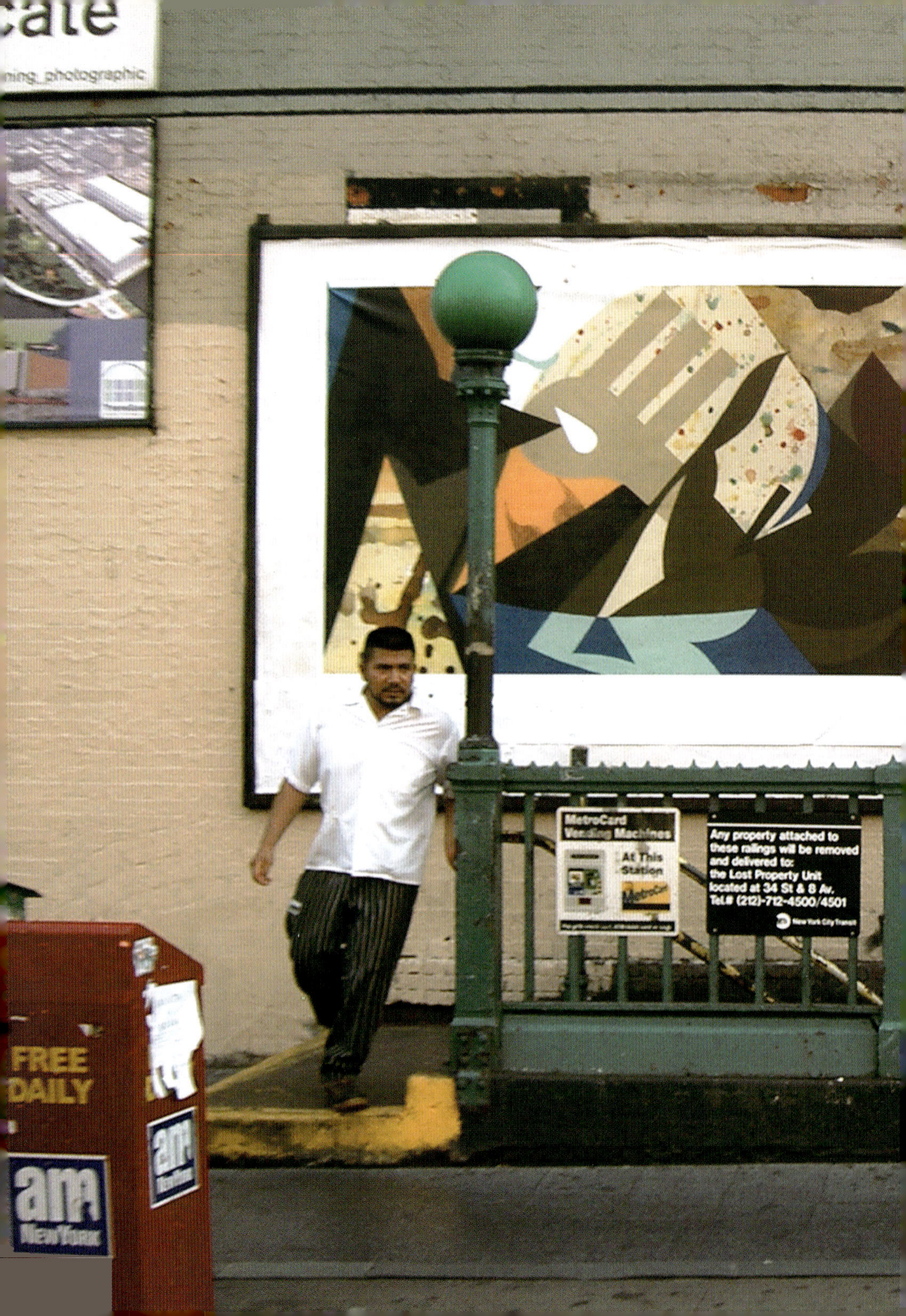
cafe
ning_photographic
MetroCard
Vending Machines
At This
Station
Any property attached to
these railings will be removed
and delivered to:
the Lost Property Unit
located at 34 St & 8 Av.
Tel.# (212)-712-4500/4501
New York City Transit
FREE
DAILY
am
New York
am

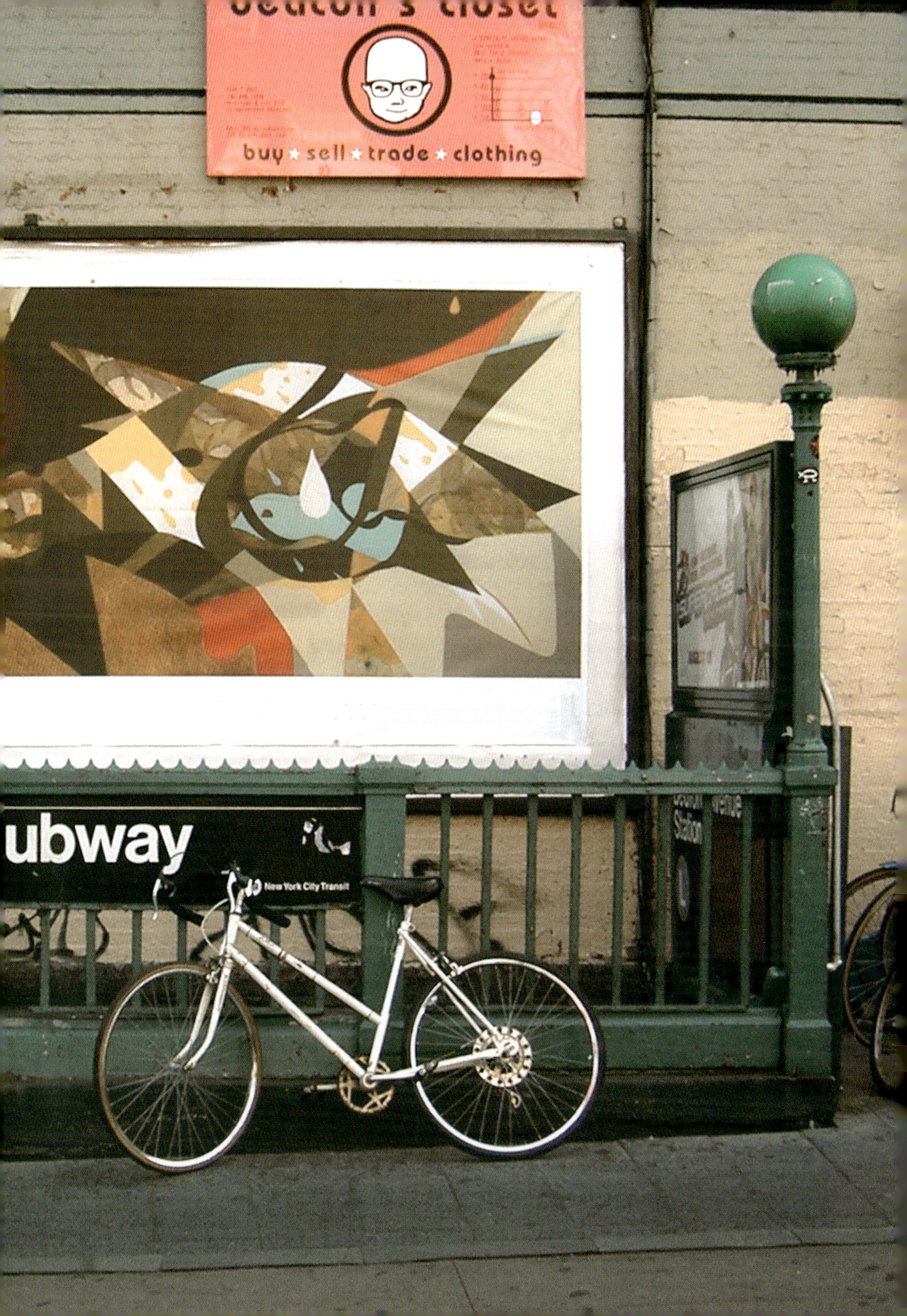
buy ⋆ sell ⋆ trade ⋆ clothing
ubway
New York City Transit

(previous page)
Fl-ye, 2005
Acrylic on paper
Billboard

(right page)
Nout, 2005
Acrylic on Canvas
2005
60 x 60"

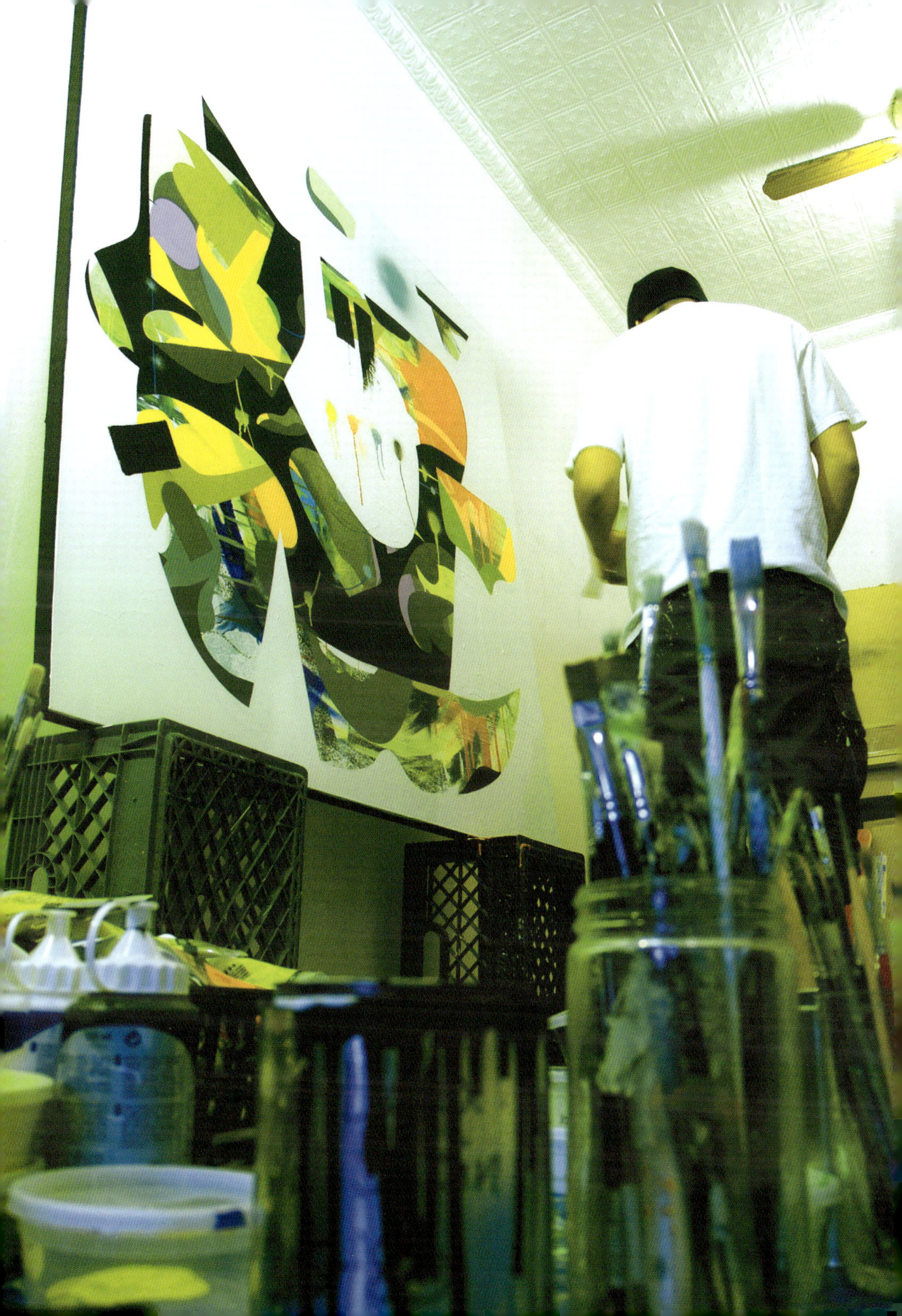

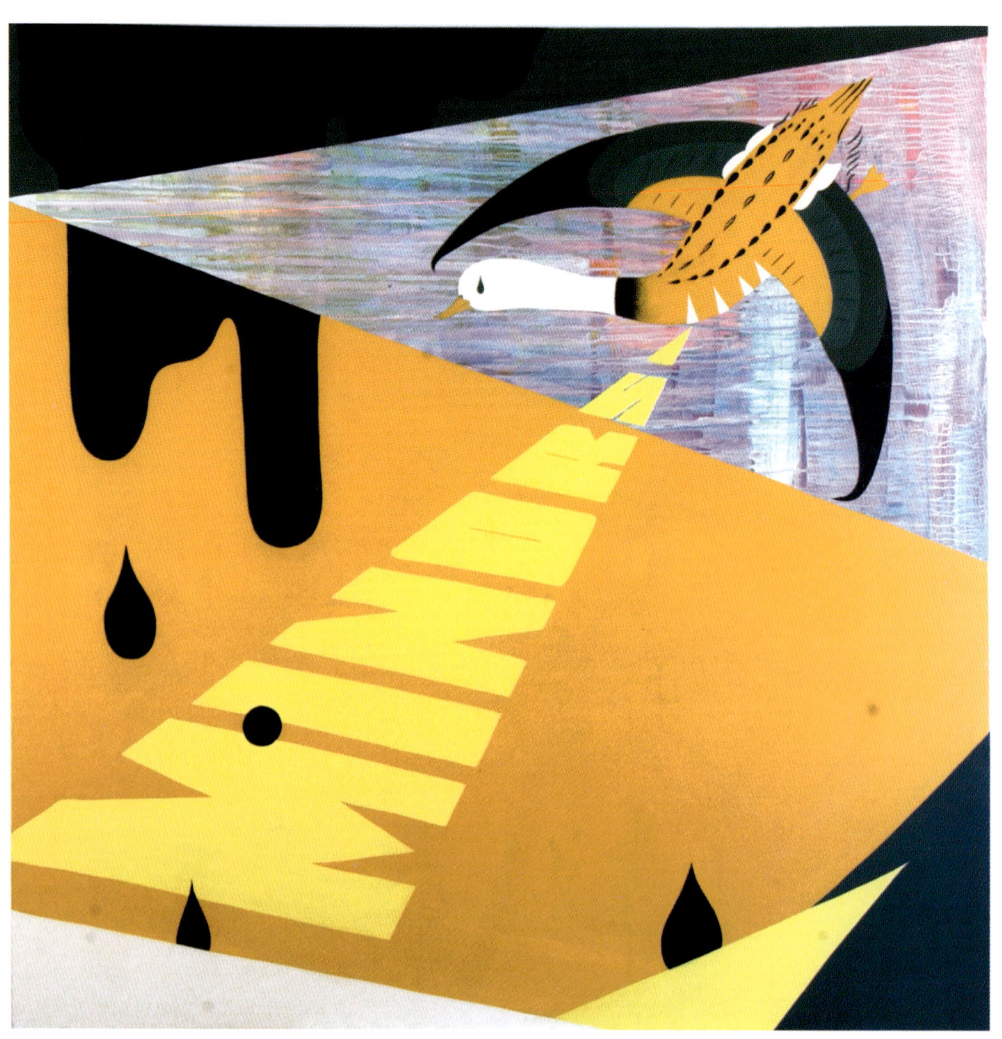

Minority, 2004
Acrylic on canvas
60 x 60"

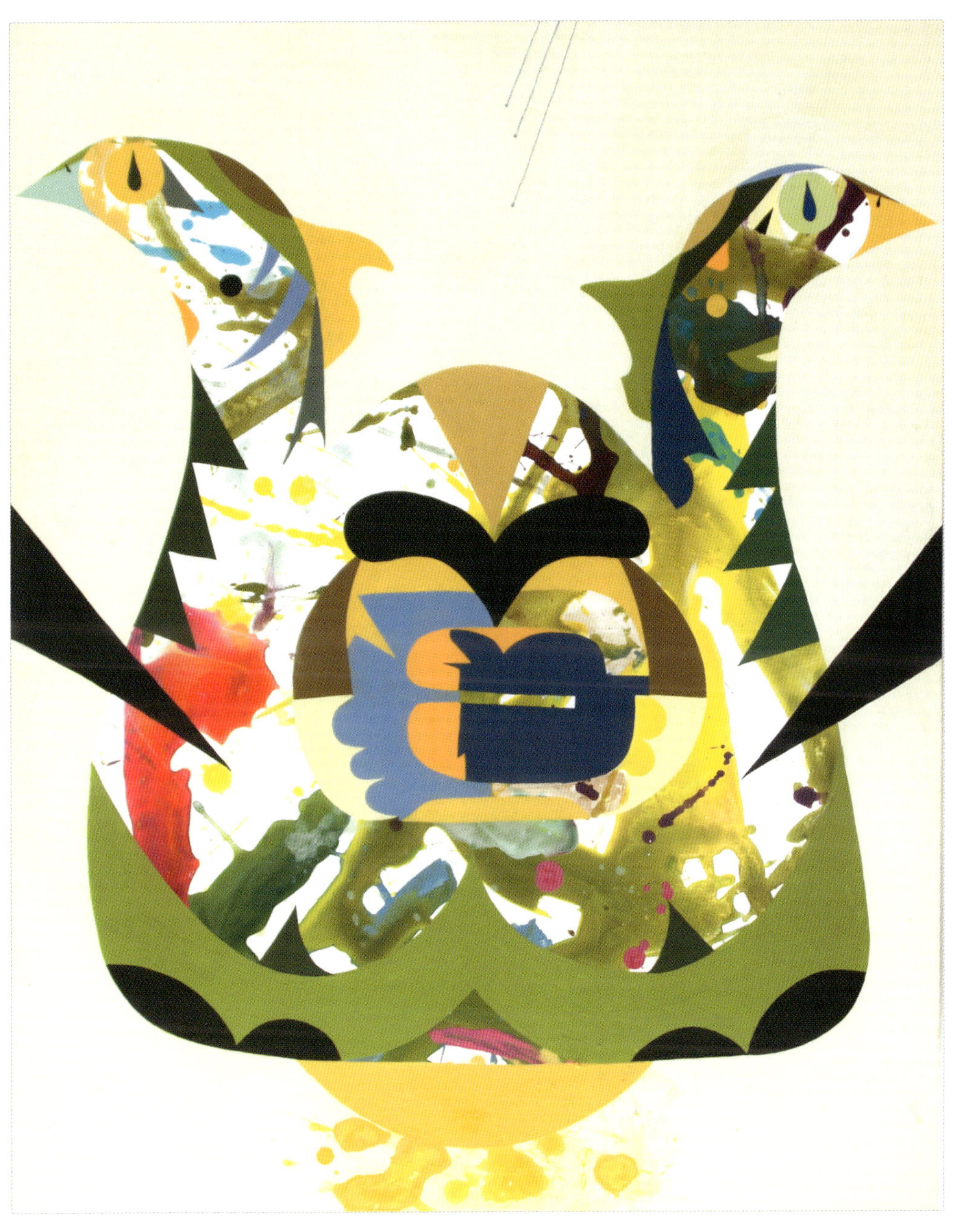

Double Tree, 2005
Acrylic on wood panel
20 x 16"

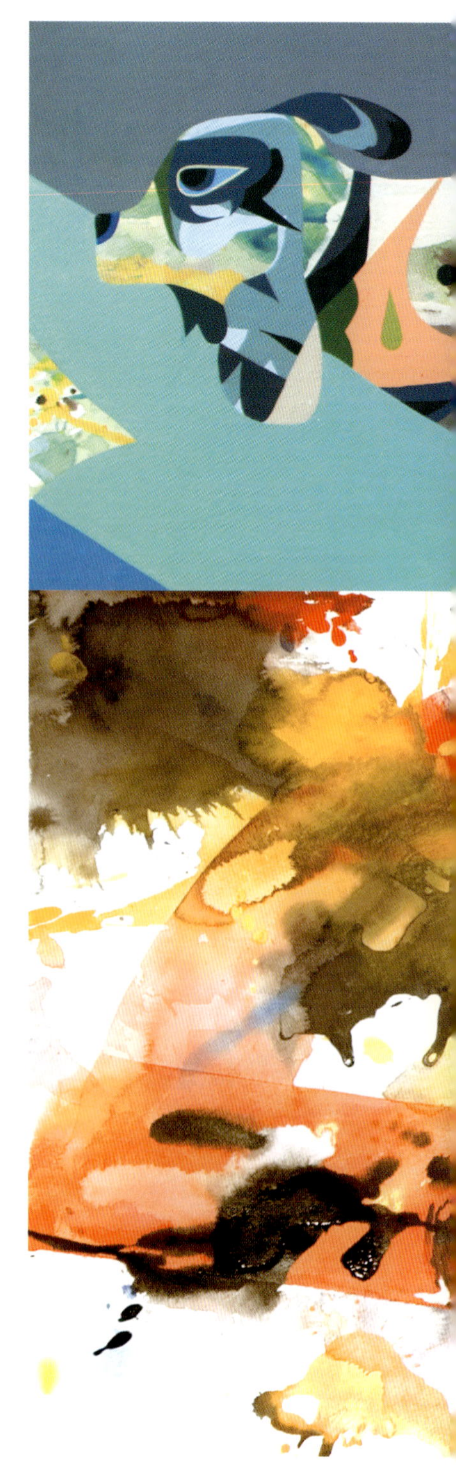

Strike Me When It's Red, 2006
Acrylic on paper
24 x 26"

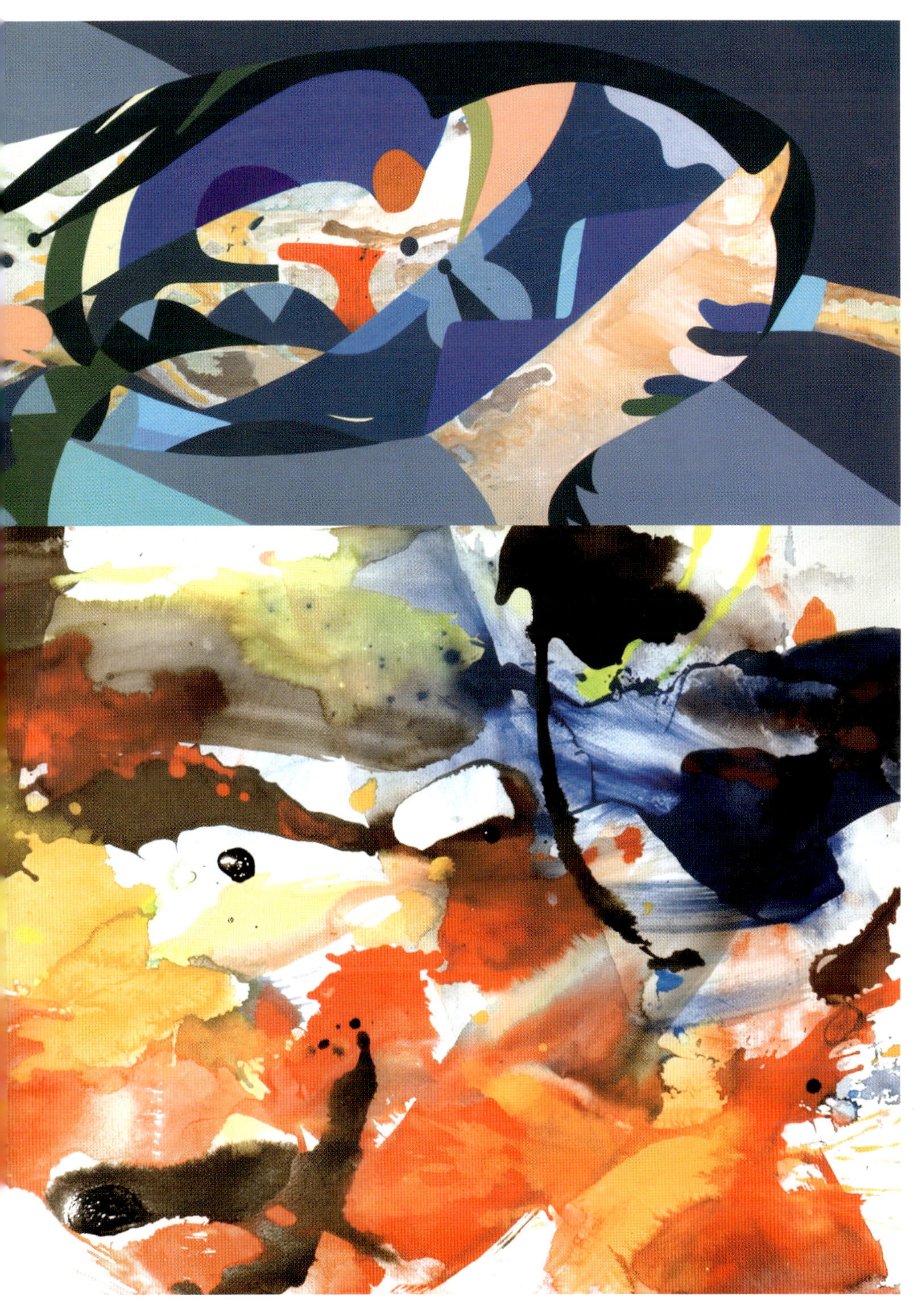

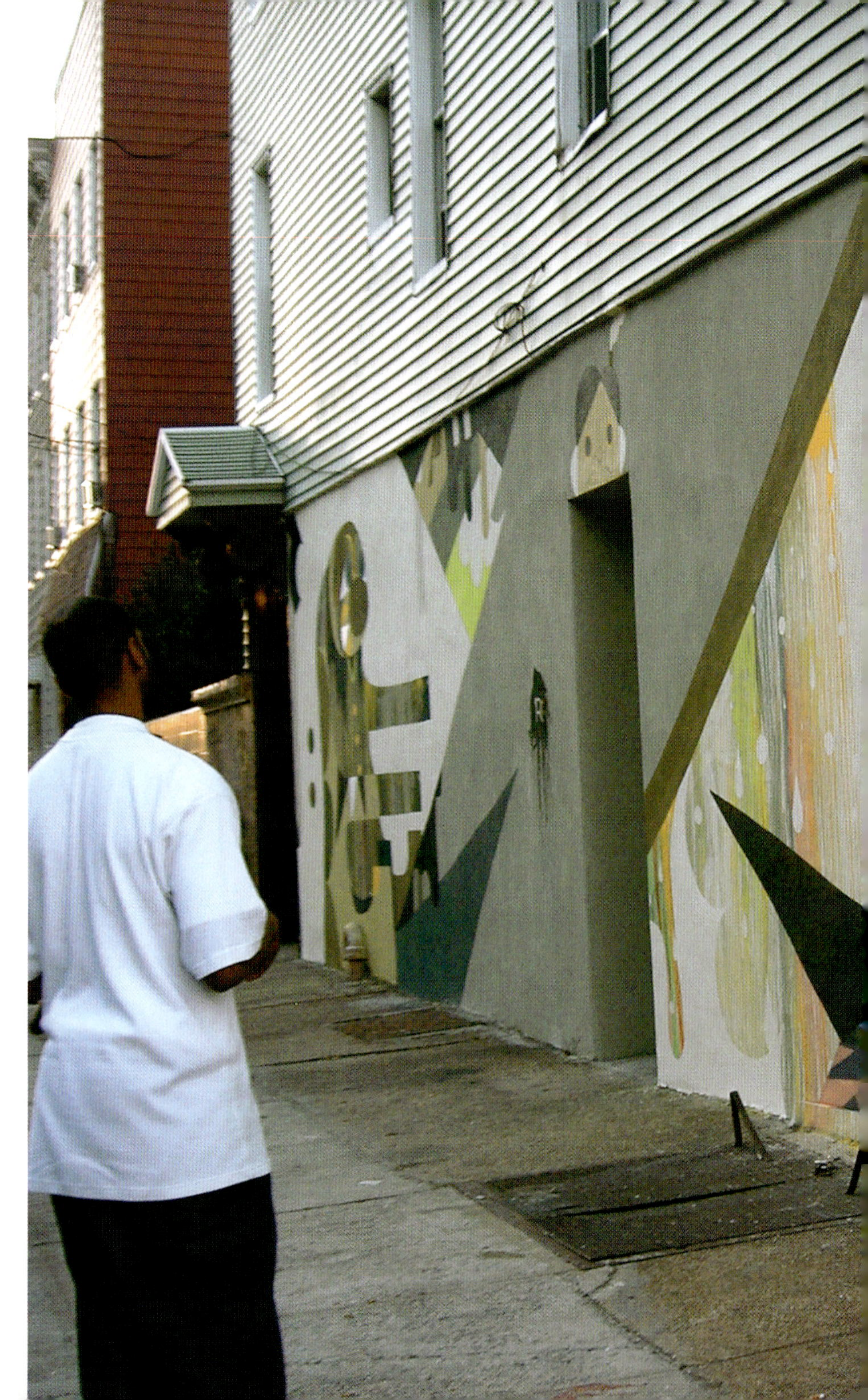

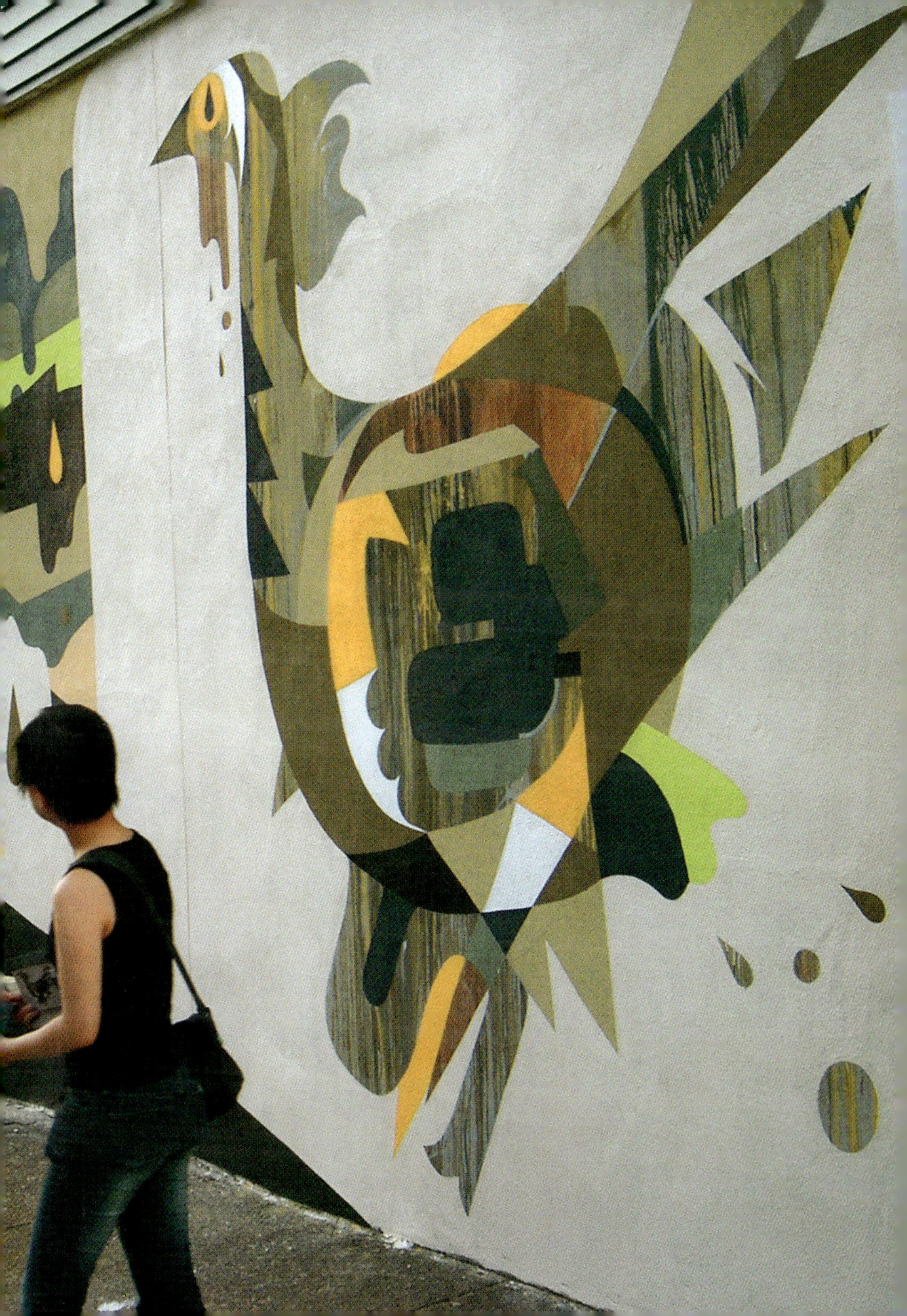

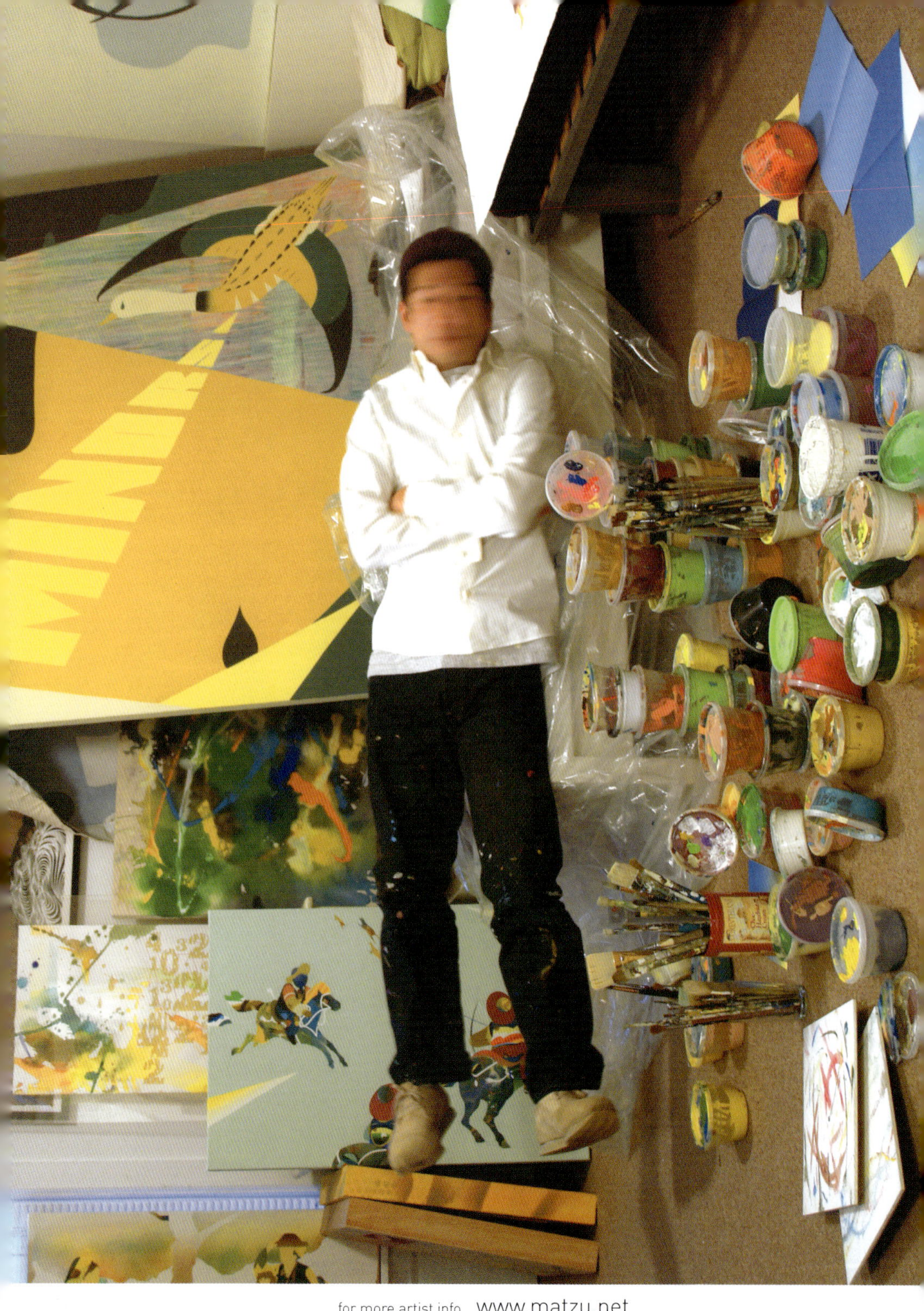

for more artist info www.matzu.net